WILLIAM

SHAKESPEARE'S

THE

JEDI DOTH RETURN

STAR WARS

PART THE SIXTH

WILLIAM

SHAKESPEARE'S

———— THE ————
JEDI DOTH RETURN

STAR WARS
PART THE SIXTH

By Ian Doescher

INSPIRED BY THE WORK OF GEORGE LUCAS
AND WILLIAM SHAKESPEARE

QUIRK BOOKS
PHILADELPHIA

Library of Congress Cataloging in Publication Number: 2013945949

ISBN: 978-1-59474-713-7

Printed in the United States of America

Typeset in Sabon

Text by Ian Doescher
Illustrations by Nicolas Delort
Production management by John J. McGurk

Quirk Books
215 Church Street
Philadelphia, PA 19106
quirkbooks.com

10 9 8 7 6 5 4 3 2 1

FOR BOB, MY DAD, WHO NE'ER CUT OFF MY HAND.

FOR BETH, MY MOM, WHO NEVER WED MY UNCLE.

AND FOR MY BROTHER ERIK, WHO NE'ER TRIED

(AS LEIA DID) TO KISS A BROTHER'S LIPS.

DRAMATIS PERSONAE

CHORUS

LUKE SKYWALKER, *a Jedi trainee*
GHOST OF OBI-WAN KENOBI, *a Jedi Knight*
YODA, *a Jedi Master*
PRINCESS LEIA ORGANA, *of Alderaan*
HAN SOLO, *a rebel captain*
CHEWBACCA, *his Wookiee and first mate*
C-3PO, *a droid*
R2-D2, *his companion*
LANDO OF CALRISSIAN, *a scoundrel*
MON MOTHMA, *leader of the Rebel Alliance*
ACKBAR AND MADINE, *rebel leaders*
WEDGE ANTILLES, *a rebel pilot*
NIEN NUNB, *a rebel pilot*
EMPEROR PALPATINE, *ruler of the Empire*
DARTH VADER, *a Sith Lord*
JERJERROD *and* PIETT, *gentlemen of the Empire*
JABBA OF THE HUTT, *a gangster*
BIB FORTUNA, *Jabba's man*
SALACIOUS CRUMB, *Jabba's fool*
BOBA FETT, *a bounty hunter*
THE MAX REBO BAND, *Jabba's palace musicians*
EV-9D9, *a droid in Jabba's service*
RANCOR, *a monster in Jabba's service*
THE RANCOR KEEPER, *its owner*

REBEL PILOTS, TROOPS, EWOKS, GAMORREAN GUARDS,
JABBA'S COURTIERS, BOUNTY HUNTERS, IMPERIAL TROOPS,
SCOUTS, OFFICERS, COMMANDERS, CONTROLLERS, GUARDS,
ROYAL GUARDS, *and* SOLDIERS

PROLOGUE.

Outer space.

Enter CHORUS.

CHORUS   O join us, friends and mortals, on the scene—
          Another chapter of our cosmic tale.
          Luke Skywalker returns to Tatooine,
          To save his friend Han Solo from his jail
          Within the grasp of Jabba of the Hutt.   5
          But while Luke doth the timely rescue scheme,
          The vile Galactic Empire now hath cut
          New plans for a space station with a beam
          More awful than the first fear'd Death Star's blast.
          This weapon ultimate shall, when complete,   10
          Mean doom for those within the rebel cast
          Who fight to earn the taste of freedom sweet.
          In time so long ago begins our play,
          In hope-fill'd galaxy far, far away.

ACT I

SCENE 1.

Inside the second Death Star.

Enter DARTH VADER *and* MOFF JERJERROD.

VADER	Cease to persuade, my grov'ling Jerjerrod,
	Long-winded Moffs have ever sniv'ling wits.
	'Tis plain to me thy progress falls behind
	And lacks the needed motivation. Thus,
	I have arriv'd to set thy schedule right. 5
JERJERROD	Aye, we are honor'd by your presence, Lord.
	To have you here is unexpected joy.
VADER	Thou mayst dispense with ev'ry pleasantry.
	Thy fawning words no int'rest hold for me.
	So cease thy prating over my arrival 10
	And tell me how thou shalt correct thy faults.
JERJERROD	I tell thee truly, Lord, my men do work
	As quickly as each one is capable—
	No more is possible for them to do.
VADER	Mayhap I shall find new, creative ways 15
	To motivate them.
JERJERROD	—Lord, I'll warrant that
	The station shall be operational
	Within the date and time that have been set.
	Upon my honor I may make such claim.
VADER	The Emperor, however, doth not share 20
	Thine optimistic attitude thereon.
JERJERROD	But, Lord, he doth expect th'impossible!
	I need more bodies to fulfill this task.
	If I had but a hundred able souls
	To work alongside those already here, 25

               'Twould be far simpler to complete the work

               And make this Death Star ready when 'tis due.

VADER   Thou wilt have opportunity to ask

               The Emp'ror for these further workers, for

               He shall arrive upon the Death Star soon.   30

JERJERROD   [*aside:*] O news that fills my heart with utter dread!

               [*To Darth Vader:*] The Emperor himself shall come

                                          here?

VADER   —Aye.

               Displeasèd is he with thy thorough lack

               Of progress on this station incomplete.

JERJERROD   Our efforts shall be doubled instantly!   35

VADER   I do hope so, Commander, for thy sake—

               The Emperor is known for being less

               Forgiving than myself. Pray, is that clear?

JERJERROD   It is, Lord Vader, perfectly. Thy words

               I hear and shall obey. With gratitude   40

               I praise thee for thine honesty herein.

                          [*Exit Moff Jerjerrod.*]

VADER   The scene is set for this, the final act.

               I shall destroy the rebels, one and all,

               And turn young Luke, my son, unto the dark.

               It is the role I play, my destiny—   45

               The grand performance for which I am made.

               Come, author of the dark side of the Force,

               Make me the servant of thy quill and write

               The tale wherein my son and I are seal'd

               As one. Come, take mine ev'ry doubt from me,   50

               And fashion from my heart of flesh and wires

               A perfect actor: callous, cold, and harsh.

               Let this, the second Death Star, be the stage,

And all the galaxy be setting to
The greatest moment of my narrative: 55
The scene in which the Empire's fight is won
Whilst I decide the Fate of mine own son.

                                        [Exit Darth Vader.

SCENE 2.

The desert planet Tatooine, at Jabba's Palace.

Enter C-3PO and R2-D2.

C-3PO   Again, R2, we are on Tatooine.
            I would not e'er have ventur'd to return
            Unto this place most desolate and wild,
            Except that Master Luke hath sent us here
            Upon an errand. Yet I know not what   5
            Our message is, but only that I should
            To Jabba of the Hutt deliver it.
            O place most barren—I have miss'd thee not.
R2-D2   Beep, squeak?
C-3PO   —Indeed I am afraid, R2,
            And so shouldst thou be, too, for Lando of   10
            Calrissian and brave Chewbacca ne'er
            Return'd from here.
R2-D2   —Beep, whistle, squeak.
C-3PO   —Be not
            So certain, R2, for if thou didst know
            But half of all that I have heard about
            This Jabba of the Hutt—his cruelty, how   15
            He tortures innocents, and all the beasts

He keeps to do his will—belike thou wouldst
Short-circuit.

R2-D2   —Hoo.

                [They approach the door of Jabba's palace.

C-3PO   —And now we have arriv'd.
But art thou sure this is the place, R2?
Mayhap 'tis best if I do knock? [*He knocks.*] Alas,   20
There's none to see us in, so let us go!

Enter GUARD DROID *on the other side of door.*

DROID   [*aside:*] Now here's a knocking, indeed! If a droid
Were porter of the Force here in this place,
He should have rust for lack of turning key.
I pray, remember the poor porter droid.   25
[*To C-3PO and R2-D2:*] N'getchoo gadda gooda,
                 einja meh.

C-3PO   My goodness! What foul greeting's this? [*To droid:*] R2-
                  D2wah.

DROID   —Haku! Danna mee bicchu.

C-3PO   Bo C-3POwah, ey.

DROID   —Ai waijay uh.

C-3PO   Odd toota mischka Jabba o du Hutt.   30

DROID   Kuju gwankee? Mypee gaza, ho ho!

C-3PO   Methinks they shall not let us in, what shame!
Still, well may it be said that we have tried,
For never would I give up easily
When sent forth on a task by Master Luke.   35
Yet we have tried and were refusèd here,
Thus, who could blame us for departing hence?
Let us depart now, aye, together fly!

                                        [The door opens.
              O pity, it doth open and release
              Mine utmost fears. Now must we venture in.   40
R2-D2   *[aside:]* My friend C-3PO was never for
              His courage known. So shall I lead, as e'er
              I have been wont to lead, into this place
              Although I too feel fear. *[To C-3PO:]* Beep, whistle,
                                              squeak!

C-3PO   O, R2, wait for me! O dear! We should   45
              Not rush, like fools, unto this scene. O my!

              Enter GAMORREAN GUARDS *and* BIB FORTUNA.

BIB   Tay chuda! Nuh die wanna wanga?
C-3PO   —O!
              Die wanna waugow. *[Translating:]* "We bring unto thy
              Dread master Jabba of the Hutt a message."
BIB   E Jabba wanga?
R2-D2   —Squeak!
C-3PO   —*[translating:]* "A gift as well."   50
              [To R2-D2:] Wait, R2, pray, what dost thou
                                          mean, "a gift"?
              Good Master Luke hath spoken not of "gift."
R2-D2   Beep, whistle, meep.
BIB   —Nee Jab' no badda; ees
              Eye oh toe. Zah kotah amutti mi'.
R2-D2   Beep, meep, nee, whistle, hoo.
C-3PO   —He doth report   55
              That we are not to give the message to
              A soul, save Jabba of the Hutt himself.
G. GUARD 1   Grrf, mik.

C-3PO   —Pray, patience; he quite stubborn is
            When fac'd with matters such as these.
BIB   —Nudd chaa!
                  [Bib Fortuna motions for the droids to follow.
C-3PO   R2, I feel a shaking in my core   60
            O'er this dread situation we are in.

Enter JABBA OF THE HUTT, BOBA FETT, THE MAX REBO BAND,
      SALACIOUS CRUMB, LANDO OF CALRISSIAN in disguise,
            and other members of Jabba's court.

JABBA   Ahho, nee jann bah naska ahho bah.
BIB   Kada no pase.
C-3PO   —Good morning.
R2-D2   —Beep, meep, squeak!
BIB   Neh bo shuhadda mana.
JABBA   —Ahh, shihu.
C-3PO   I prithee, R2, play the message now.   65
            The sooner we'll be on our merry way.
JABBA   Bo shuda!
R2-D2   —Beep, meep, whistle.

            Enter LUKE SKYWALKER, in beam.

LUKE   —Greetings, O
            Exalted Jabba of the Hutt. Allow
            Me to make introduction unto thee:
            My name is Luke Skywalker, Jedi Knight   70
            And friend to Captain Solo, who e'en now
            Is in thy custody. I know that thou
            Art powerful, O Jabba, and that thy

Great anger t'ward Han Solo equally
Must pow'rful be. I seek an audience   75
With thy esteem'd and mighty personage,
To bargain for my friend Han Solo's life.
With thy vast wisdom we shall, doubtless, find
A goodly compromise that shall, indeed,
Be mutually beneficial, and   80
Allow both you and I to 'scape a more
Unpleasant confrontation. As a sign
And symbol of my honest will, I do
Present unto thee, as a gift, these droids.

	They are hardworking, and shall serve thee well.	85
C-3PO	Alas, what hath he said?	
R2-D2	—Beep, whistle, meep!	
C-3PO	Nay, nay! R2, I say, your message errs!	
	Our master never would betray us so!	
CRUMB	O foolish droids, whose master fools them so!	
BIB	[to Jabba:] Na maska bagweni, ees no Jedi.	90
JABBA	Ha ono wangee goghpah, ool.	
C-3PO	—We're doom'd!	
	He will not bargain with good Master Luke.	
JABBA	Nuh peecha wangee cogh pah, tong nam nee	
	Took chan kee troi. Ne Solo fah keechwa.	
C-3PO	O, R2, look, 'tis Captain Solo, still	95
	A'frozen in the carbonite.	
R2-D2	—Beep, hoo!	
CRUMB	A little more than dud and less than dead.	
JABBA	Na pushka nab, de foghla pah nubin!	

Enter EV-9D9, *a droid, as Gamorrean guards lead*
C-3PO *and* R2-D2 *to him.*

C-3PO	O what hath come upon my master Luke?	
	Did I offend him by some errant word?	100
	Was he disturb'd by something I have said?	
	Or is this but a human's changing whim?	
	Belike I'll never fully comprehend	
	These people and their wayward, shifting ways.	
	One moment with my service is he pleas'd,	105
	The next he sendeth me away in scorn	
	To serve the gangster Jabba of the Hutt.	
	Grant me thy mercy, Sir, I beg of thee—	

Whatever my offense, O master true,
I prithee, do forgive C-3PO! 110

R2-D2 [*aside:*] What scenes of horror lie herein! I see
That droids are tortur'd here, fix'd fast upon
The rack and torn to bits, or burnèd on
The feet as though they were a piece of meat
Upon a spit. O terror to mine eyes— 115
And yet I know my master hath a plan.
Indeed, within my head I hold the light
That shall illumine our profound escape.

EV-9D9 New acquisitions, excellent. Thou art
A droid of protocol: say, is this so? 120

C-3PO I am C-3PO, of human—

EV-9D9   —Aye,
Or nay shall serve.

C-3PO   —O. Aye.

EV-9D9   —Of languages,
How many dost thou speak?

C-3P   —Six million forms
Of speech I may claim knowledge of—

EV-9D9   —'Tis well.
We have not had a court interpreter 125
Since our great master anger'd was by our
Most recent droid of protocol, and had
Him thoroughly disintegrated.

C-3PO   —O!
Disintegrated? Fate most vile and cruel!

EV-9D9 I prithee, guard, this droid of protocol 130
May useful be. Take him and fit him with
A strong restraining bolt, and then return
Him unto our great master's chamber.

G. GUARD 2   —Mrk.

C-3PO   O, R2, do not leave me all alone!

                   [Gamorrean Guard 2 leads C-3PO
                        back to Jabba of the Hutt.

R2-D2   Beep, squeak!

EV-9D9   —Thou art a feisty little droid,   135
             But soon shall learn respect when thou dost serve
             Upon my master's sail barge. Thou shalt see!

                        [Exeunt EV-9D9 and R2-D2.

C-3PO   *[aside:]* Within the court of Jabba now I serve.
             But O, what wretched things I see within,
             For when he loseth temper—which befalls   140
             Most frequently—thou mayst be certain it
             Doth mean the death of someone who is nigh.
             For lo, unto the rancor's pit they fall,
             Where such a massive terror lives that I
             Cannot bear watch, though all the courtiers here   145
             Do laugh and cheer as though it were a sport.
             The rancor cometh forth with growls and barks
             And catches up the poor and helpless soul
             Who, screaming in its terror, doth fall mute
             As rancor sinks large teeth into its flesh.   150
             The slaughter of the blameless! O, it is
             A vile and filthy service I fulfill.
             Grant me the patience to endure this time!

                        [The Max Rebo Band plays a song of
                             tribute to Jabba of the Hutt.

REBO BAND   *[sings:]* A gangster, aye, a gangster, O!
             'Tis well to be a gangster.   155
             A blaster ever by thy side,
             A stately barge in which to ride,

A fair, young damsel to thee tied,
'Tis well to be a gangster.
A gangster, aye, a gangster, O!   160
'Tis well to be a gangster.
Full many servants lend thee aid,
More guards than a Naboo brigade,
And bounty hunters on parade—
'Tis well to be a gangster.   165
A gangster, aye, a gangster, O!
'Tis well to be a gangster.
The drinks all flowing fast and free,
A sarlacc pit not far from thee,
A rancor for thine enemy,   170
'Tis well to be a gangster.
A gangster, aye, a gangster, O!
'Tis well to be a gangster.

A blast is heard. Enter CHEWBACCA *and*
BOUSHH, *a bounty hunter.*

BOUSHH   Eyah-tay, eyah-tay, yo-toe.
C-3PO   —Chewbacca!
CHEWBAC.   —Auugh!
JABBA   Cheesa eejah wahkee Chewbacca—ho!   175
FETT   [*aside*:] The Wookiee hath been captur'd—e'en
            he who with my grand prize Solo once did fly.
            'Tis fortunate he hath to Jabba also been deliver'd.
            I only wish that I had been his captor, and reap'd
            the reward this bounty hunter surely shall receive.   180
            Even so, this Wookiee doth complete the set of
            smugglers for Jabba's merriment. Belike he too
            shall frozen in carbonite be, or mayhap be a
            supper for a rancor.
JABBA   Kahjee ta, droid.
C-3PO   —Aye, here am I, indeed,   185
            Thy worshipfulness.
JABBA   —Yu-bahk ko rahto
            Kama wahl-bahk. Eye yess ka cho. Kawa
            Na Wookiee.
C-3PO   —Bounty hunter strong and brave:
            The mighty Jabba of the Hutt doth bid
            Thee welcome, and shall gladly pay to thee   190
            The goodly sum of five-and-twenty thousand.
CRUMB   [*aside*:] No bounty hunter would be fool enough
            To take the first price offer'd, I'll be sworn.
BOUSHH   Yoto. Yoto.
C-3PO   —'Tis fifty thousand, and
            No less.

JABBA	[*striking C-3PO:*] —Ahh, uun yun kuss tah fiti pun. 195
C-3PO	Whatever was it that I said, Sirrah?
	I did perform the function thou hast giv'n:
	Precisely did I translate this one's words.
JABBA	Moonon keejo!
FETT	[*aside:*] This scamp had best beware, if
	he would be a bounty hunter in the service of 200
	great Jabba. It seemeth he hath little appreciation
	for the famèd anger of the Hutt.
C-3PO	[*to Boushh:*] —The mighty Jabba asks
	The reason wherefore fifty thousand is
	The sum demanded of thee.
BOUSHH	—Ay yo-toe! 205
C-3PO	The knave doth threaten us—he holdeth in
	His hands a thermal detonator. O!
	[*Jabba's courtiers shrink in fear.*
	Boba Fett takes out his blaster.
JABBA	Ho, ho. Kaso ya yee koli tra do
	Kahn nee go. Yu bahn chuna leepa nah.
CRUMB	The Hutt doth call him fearless and inventive, 210
	But never did invention make me fear
	As this one's thermal detonator doth.
JABBA	[*to C-3PO:*] Kuo meeta tah te fye. Dah tee teema
	Nye.
C-3PO	[*to Boushh:*] —Mighty Jabba offers thirty-five,
	And were I in thy place, I would accept 215
	The deal. 'Tis better, as they say, to make
	The peace than make us all in pieces be.
	And truly thirty-five while living is
	A sum more numerous than zero dead.
BOUSHH	Ya-toe cha.

C-3PO   —Praise the maker, he agrees!   220
CHEWBAC.   Auugh!

> [*Chewbacca is led away by Gamorrean*
> *guards as music begins to play again.*

LANDO   [*aside:*]   —This sad scene I witness with contempt:
           Another bounty hunter earns his sum
           For bringing in a harmless innocent.
           Now all is merriment and patting on
           The back whilst yet another's added to   225
           Their clan. A scoundrel's life 'tis true I've known,
           Yet never did I stoop so low as this.
           But still, I smile at what I here survey,
           For I know well this bounty hunter is
           No normal man—no normal man indeed!   230
           And his apparent prize—my Wookiee friend
           Chewbacca—is not as a pris'ner come.
           Bear thou this burden bravely, Lando, for
           The wait is almost over—soon the plan
           O'er which we took great pains shall come to pass.   235
           Be still, my scoundrel heart, with patience wait,
           For retribution comes in time, though late.

> [*Exeunt.*

SCENE 3.

The desert planet Tatooine, at Jabba's Palace. Night.

Enter BOUSHH.

BOUSHH   The silence of the night doth mark my work
           And like a gentle breeze sweeps o'er the air.

In stealth I move throughout the palace dark,
That no one shall bear witness to my acts.
Now cross the court, with footsteps nimbly plac'd.   5
Ne'er did a matter of such weight depend
Upon a gentle footfall in the night.
Put out the light, and then relume his light—
Aye, now I spy my goal: the frozen Han.
Thy work is finish'd, feet. Now 'tis the hands   10
That shall a more profound task undertake.
Quick to the panel, press the needed code.
O swiftly fly, good hands, and free this man
From his most cold and undeservèd cell.
O true decryptionist, thy codes are quick!   15
The scheme hath work'd, the carbonite doth melt.
Forsooth, 'tis done—within the silent dark
The greatest light doth sing within my heart!

                    [Han Solo melts from the carbonite
                                and falls to the floor.

[*To Han Solo:*] Relax thou for a moment; thou art free
Of carbonite's embrace, but thou dost burn   20
From this harsh hibernation malady.

HAN	I cannot see.
BOUSHH	—Thine eyesight shall return.
HAN	But where am I?
BOUSHH	—In Jabba's Palace you
	Have been detain'd.
HAN	—Who art thou, voice severe?

        [Boushh removes his mask to reveal Princess Leia.

LEIA	The one whose heart and soul do love thee true.	25
HAN	O, Leia!	

                               [They kiss.

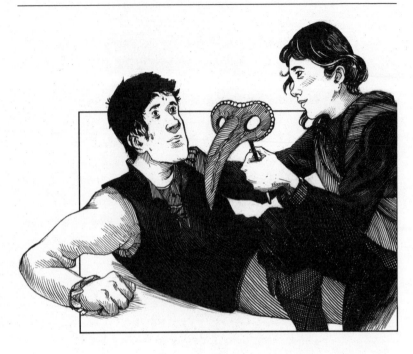

LEIA   —Come, and let's away from here.

Enter JABBA OF THE HUTT, BIB FORTUNA, BOBA FETT,
THE MAX REBO BAND, SALACIOUS CRUMB, LANDO OF CALRISSIAN
in disguise, and other members of Jabba's court.

JABBA   Ho, ho, ho.
HAN   —O, that laugh, it works me woe.
            'Tis too familiar in my memory,
            And like a chime from Hell's forsaken bells
            Doth ring most evilly within mine ears.   30
JABBA   Oofila mooga bos.
HAN   —Pray, Jabba, see:
            I was upon my way to pay thee back,
            And in returning happen'd on a course

	That ran the other way. 'Tis not my fault.
JABBA	Achi pahbuk moonitnuh, Solo, bah. 35
	Akingsah rebah bachmanah bakmah
	Jaja weetnowah bantha poodoo, ho!
CRUMB	He shall be bantha fodder, O, 'tis true—
	A Solo may make progress through the guts
	Of banthas! Aye, my master's passing wise. 40
HAN	I'll pay thee triple, Jabba, thou canst not
	Deny this fortune—be thou not a fool!

[Han Solo is taken away by guards.

| JABBA | Nakko, kosleeya ni. |

[Guards take Princess Leia to Jabba.

LEIA	—Now shall I be
	His plaything? [To Jabba:] We have friends most
	powerful.
	Thou shalt, with all thy heart, regret this act. 45
JABBA	Bana madota, heah.
C-3PO	—Why were my eyes
	E'er made to see, when such as this must be
	Within my sight? I cannot bear to watch.

[Exeunt Jabba's court.

Enter HAN SOLO and CHEWBACCA on balcony, as their cell.

HAN	What fate is this? What curs'd, unearnèd path?
	Within a minute rescu'd by my love, 50
	Then taken from her unto this grim place.
	How long was I in carbonite encas'd?
	Am I an old man now, with graying hair?
	What jubilant occasions have I miss'd?
	What friends have died, or have been lost fore'er? 55

Hath our Rebellion disappointed been,
Or is it now fulfill'd with all success?
Because I do not know how long I've slept,
Or what transpir'd while I was frozen thus,
It seems my mind is sluggish to defrost.   60

CHEWBAC. Grrm.

HAN   —Yet another sound familiar, but
This one doth bring delight into my soul.
Chewbacca? Prithee, tell me, Chewie, is
It thou who art here with me?

CHEWBAC.   —Auugh.

HAN   —Sweet joy!
What bounty of affection do I feel   65
For thee, dear Wookiee. I cannot yet see,
But knowing thou art here doth warm my heart.
I prithee, give me news of all that is.

CHEWBAC. Egh, auugh!

HAN   —What sayst thou? Luke—a Jedi Knight?
What strange tomfoolery! Luke is but young,   70
Not made for rescues.

CHEWBAC.   —Auugh!

HAN   —Thou dost report
I have been gone a time but fleeting, so
Have all acquir'd delusions of some grandeur?
And what of Han? Have I been left behind?
O thought most base, O destiny unkind.   75

                                        [Exeunt.

SCENE 4.

The desert planet Tatooine, at Jabba's Palace.

Enter LUKE SKYWALKER.

LUKE   The time is now, the place is here, the man
              Myself, the matter: rescue of my friends.
              Be focus'd, mind; be settl'd, heart and soul.
              I enter unto Jabba's palace for
              One purpose and that purpose by itself: 5
              My friends to find and bring deliverance.
              Now to it, Luke, and earn the Jedi name,
              Not by thy might, but by thy calm and wit.

Enter BIB FORTUNA.

BIB   Yo mot tu cheep, do you pan Skywalker.
              Nuh Jabba mo bah toe baht too.
LUKE   —Nay, Sir.   10
              I tell thee: I shall speak with Jabba now.
BIB   Nuh Jabba no two zand dehank obee.
                        [*Luke uses a Jedi mind trick on Bib Fortuna.*
LUKE   Thou shalt take me to Jabba presently.
BIB   Naja takka to Jabba prekkenlee.
LUKE   Thou servest thy proud master well, and shall,   15
              In time, receive from him a great reward.
BIB   Eye sota y'locha. Ba chu noya trot.

Enter JABBA OF THE HUTT, PRINCESS LEIA, C-3PO, BOBA FETT,
THE MAX REBO BAND, SALACIOUS CRUMB, LANDO OF CALRISSIAN
in disguise, and other members of Jabba's court.

LUKE	[*aside:*] Say what is this? My Leia sparsely clad
	All in a metal-fashion'd suit? How strange!
	I did expect one of our company 20
	To be enclos'd in steel, but not like this.
C-3PO	At last, 'tis Master Luke to rescue us!
BIB	[*to Jabba:*] Nuh masta, gabba no pace Skywalker.
JABBA	Nah mass fa wong lee fah toon kay.
LUKE	—Thou must,
	Great Jabba, grant me leave to speak with thee. 25
BIB	Nuh Jedi modst be inco ee, baanah.
CRUMB	Old Bib but echoes what the man doth say!
JABBA	Ahh, ko ja vaya sko. Ees turo na
	Om Jedi mine chik.

> *[Jabba strikes Bib Fortuna, who falls.*

LUKE	—Let me be plain:
	Thou shalt with all expedience produce 30
	Both Captain Solo and the Wookiee, and
	Shall grant our safe departure from this place.
	'Tis this, and nothing more, I shall accept.
JABBA	Ya ku kacha ka puna ni sa. Ee?
LUKE	My Jedi powers may not work on thee, 35
	But still I shall take Captain Solo and
	His friends. Thou canst yet choose to profit from
	This plan, or be destroy'd. It is thy choice,
	But thou art warn'd: to underestimate
	My pow'r would bring about thy end at once. 40
C-3PO	But Master Luke, thou standest on—
JABBA	—Ban gon
	Wah she co, cah O Jedi. Cho kanya _____
	Wee shaja keecho, ho!

> *[Luke uses the Force to take a blaster from a guard.*

                       Ah bahloosku!
            [Jabba presses a button that drops Luke and
                Gamorrean Guard 2 into the rancor pit.

CRUMB   Now shall we see the rancor rancorous!

         Enter RANCOR *into the pit with Luke and*
             the Gamorrean guard.

LANDO   [*aside:*] Alas, now Luke is thrown into the pit—   45
               His skill must see him through. My part shall be
               To give protection to the princess now.

C-3PO   For pity—now the monster hideous
               Hath come forth from his hiding place to sup.

RANCOR   [*sings:*] They shriek at my mystique,   50
               My teeth they'll die beneath—
               A feast made for a beast,
               A treat that I may eat!

LUKE   What terrifying creature-thing is this?
               Ne'er have I such a ghastly being seen.   55
               But still these thoughts, for succor have they none:
               Be calm now, Luke, or else—sans doubt—you die.

G. GUARD 2 Squeal!

LEIA   —That poor guard shall be the first to fall,
               For he doth panic and is cornerèd.
               The rancor slowly makes his way t'ward him   60
               And sees his dinner spread before his eyes.

C-3PO   O wretched beast! He tears the guard apart
               With sound of breaking bones and crumpl'd flesh.
               One need not know six million language forms
               To understand the screams and sudden hush.   65

CRUMB   It shall be time to hire another guard!

RANCOR   [*sings:*] The fat one now is flat,
              He growls within me bow'ls,
              And yet I'll not forget
              To source my second course.   70

LUKE   He turns in my direction, counting on
              His next delicious morsel to be ta'en
              E'en from my body. Aye, he cometh quick!
              This stick shall my protection be—we'll see
              If he hath appetite for wooded grains.   75

LANDO   [*aside:*] Luke now is in its grasp, but cunningly
              Hath bought a little time, and put a log
              Inside the creature's mouth. Fight on, good Luke!

LEIA   Well done, dear friend. Anon, make haste and flee!

RANCOR   [*sings:*] The one doth quickly run,   80
              I'll catch him—down the hatch him!
              The stick's a nasty trick—
              His head shall be my bread.

LUKE   Now swiftly through the monster's legs I fly,
              For yonder, past the creature, lies a door!   85
              On reaching it, I shall make my escape.
                              [*Luke attempts to open the door.*
              Alas, but what is this? More bars behind
              The door!

C-3PO   —O Master, find another course!

LUKE   'Tis just the beast and I. But look, how he
              Doth come toward me through the very gate   90
              Whence first he came. If I could close the gate
              On him, he shall be slain. Aye, here's a rock,
              And there's the panel for the door's control.
              'Tis now or ne'er. I call upon the Force
              To guide this rock unto the very spot.   95

LEIA His plan hath been reveal'd—O clever Luke!
The rock he throweth straight and hits the mark—
The gate doth fall, the rancor is destroy'd!
O brave escape, O clever, daring Luke!

JABBA Nuh toota ah! Gungsh Solo nuh Wookiee! 100
Takootay noota bangass nuh baskah.

CRUMB My master's plaything cunningly dispos'd—
If Jabba shall not play, he'll make them pay.

Enter the RANCOR KEEPER, *as Luke is
taken back to Jabba's court.*

R. KEEPER O that this too, too sullied flesh would melt
Into oblivion, if I without 105
My pet belov'd must live. O darkest world!
O misery beyond compare to me.
Already my beast's life doth play its part
Within the tend'rest mem'ries of my brain.
How well I do remember when the beast 110
Was but a rancor pup. It was the runt—
Was almost eaten by its mother cruel—
Indeed, it had but little chance for life.
Yet it was purchas'd as a novelty
By Jawas who e'er seek abnormal things. 115
I bought it from this band of Jawas, who
Related to me all it had been through
And chargèd me a paltry sum for such
A worthy animal. Then did I raise
It from its lowly start unto the grand 120
And tow'ring hulk that now before me lies.
How fondly I recall the playful nips

It gave me, which eventually turn'd
To bites that drew no small amount of blood.
I train'd it to be vicious, to enjoy   125
The taste of flesh and powd'ry crunch of bone.
Yet ever did it know its master true—
And never would it turn its anger fierce
Upon the one who lov'd it first and best.
Was ever rancor in this humor rais'd?   130
Was ever rancor in this humor won?
To think on it brings pain past all resolve.
O Fate, that ever I should see this day—
Now there's but little light left in this world,
For its bright sun unjustly is snuff'd out.   135
I shall away, and drown myself in tears,
Belike to live the sad remainder of
My mortal days upon this planet grave
Unfriended, unprotected, and alone.

                           [Exit rancor keeper.

Enter HAN SOLO *and* CHEWBACCA, *escorted by* GUARDS.

LUKE   O Han!
HAN   —'Tis Luke?
LUKE   —How dost thou fare, good friend?   140
      Thou art less cold than when I saw thee last.
HAN   The ice hath gone, but still the chill remains.
      But I am well enough, consid'ring all,
      And now we are together once again.
LUKE   'Twould not be miss'd. Such fun we have in store.   145
HAN   How is our cause?
LUKE   —The same as ever, friend.

HAN   That bad, indeed? And where is Leia?

LEIA   —Here.

I am quite safe and, as of yet, unharm'd,

But bound unto this wormlike lump of hate.

JABBA   Hagoy ooneetonuh.

C-3PO   —O dear! The great   150

And high exaltedness, this Jabba of

The Hutt, decrees that ye shall presently

Be terminated.

HAN   —Just as well; I loathe

A lengthy wait. [*Aside:*] The eyes may yet be blind,

But 'tis relief to know the wit is well.   155

C-3PO   Thou shalt, therefore, be ta'en to the Dune Sea,

And cast into the pit of old Carkoon,

The nesting place of the all-pow'rful sarlacc.

HAN   As yet this Fate doth not so dismal sound.

CRUMB   [*aside:*] I lik'd him better when he was on ice—   160

The frozen one hath quite a shrewish mouth.

Belike the details of the sarlacc shall

Give rest to his most flippant, prating tongue.

C-3PO   Within the sarlacc's belly ye shall know

A definition new of suffering   165

As ye are gradu'lly digested o'er

A thousand thousand years. Thus saith the Hutt.

HAN   As I reflect, mayhap we should decline.

I find I have no stomach for this feast

Since it is we who shall the supper be.   170

CHEWBAC.   Auugh!

LUKE   —Thou wilt soon regret this gross mistake,

For 'tis the last misstep thou e'er shalt make.

                               [*Exeunt.*

SCENE 5.

The desert planet Tatooine, at the sarlacc's pit in the Dune Sea.

Enter R2-D2 on Jabba's barge.

R2-D2   The end of this bleak scene is almost near,
             For I shall play the part of helpmate to
             My master true, securing freedom for
             Us all. No more shall Jabba terrorize
             The planet Tatooine, for he shall be   5
             Destroy'd before the double sun doth set.

Enter C-3PO, bumping into R2-D2.

C-3PO   O pardon me, I do apologize.
R2-D2   Beep, squeak!
C-3PO   —My R2, ah! What dost thou here?
R2-D2   Beep, whistle, meep, beep, nee!
C-3PO   —Well can I see
             That thou art serving drinks, but dangerous   10
             This place is. Soon they plan to execute
             Good Master Luke, and if we take not care,
             No doubt we shall be executed too!
R2-D2   Beep, meep!
C-3PO   —I wish I had thy confidence.

Enter LUKE SKYWALKER, HAN SOLO, *and* CHEWBACCA *with*
LANDO OF CALRISSIAN *in disguise and several* GUARDS
on balcony, as Jabba's skiff.

LUKE   [*aside:*] Here is the hour that ends in our escape,   15
              Here is the moment Jabba sees defeat,
              Here is the instant I have plannèd for,
              Here is the battle grand: the skiff's the thing
              Wherein I'll catch Han's rescue and take wing.

HAN   Methinks mine eyes have quite improv'd, for now   20
              Instead of just a blur of dark I see
              A blur of light. 'Tis almost pleasant. Ha!

LUKE   Alas, 'tis nothing here to see. I did
              Once live on Tatooine, as thou dost know.

HAN   And thou shalt die here too. Convenient 'tis.   25

LUKE   Stay close to Lando and Chewbacca. All
              Things shall end well, for I have plann'd it so.

HAN   So sayest thou. [*Aside:*] His confidence is such
             As I've not seen in him before; I know
             Not whether to guffaw or be impress'd.   30
                          [*Guards extend the skiff's plank
                          and force Luke onto it.*

LUKE   The plank hath been set forth, and I shall walk
             Not unto death, but our deliverance.

Enter JABBA OF THE HUTT, PRINCESS LEIA *bound to Jabba,* BIB
FORTUNA, BOBA FETT, THE MAX REBO BAND, SALACIOUS CRUMB,
and other members of Jabba's court below, on a barge.

JABBA   Koneetah!
C-3PO   —Hear ye! Victims of the great
             Almighty sarlacc: Jabba of the Hutt,
             His excellency, hopeth ye shall die   35
             With honor. Should ye wish for mercy now
             To beg, great Jabba of the Hutt shall hear
             Your pleas.
HAN   —Nay, 3PO! Say thou to that
             Vast slimy piece of filth bestrewn with worms
             He shall have no such pleasure out of us!   40
             Now that I am no more a markèd man,
             I shall most fully proffer my belief
             That Jabba is a horrid murderer
             Far worse than any I have ever known.
             Who here shall prove me wrong or argue, eh?   45
             'Tis right, good Chewie, I speak true?
CHEWBAC.   —Egh, auugh!
LUKE   Pray, Jabba, hear: I shall not ask again—
             Thou mayst free us, or be destroy'd anon.

	So give us liberty or give thyself death.	
JABBA	Ho, ho! Sabutah mayr.	
CRUMB	—Aye, put him in!	50
	No more of these fools' speech my ears would hear!	
LUKE	[*aside:*] The scene is set. Pray, Lando, play thy part,	
	And R2, thou hast ever been most true,	
	Now fail me not in this most vital time.	
R2-D2	[*aside:*] This is the moment; aye, this is the time.	55
JABBA	Koos nooma!	
CRUMB	—Let the suffering begin!	
	I shall enjoy this show of pain and death.	
LEIA	Alas, Luke jumps! But wait, he flips aright	
	Onto the skiff, and R2 hath releas'd	
	Into the air Luke's lightsaber! He has't,	60
	'Tis his! O clever droid, with aim so true,	
	And clever Luke, devising such a plan.	
HAN	The battle's here! Mine eyes see well enough	
	To know that now 'tis time for combat!	
CHEWBAC.	—Auugh!	
LANDO	Now, Lando, to thy recompense for all	65
	That thou hast done! Betrayer shall become	
	The bravest fighter e'er rebellion's seen!	
	My courage here shall render payment for	
	The villainy I've tender'd in the past.	

[They battle, and many of Jabba's court
are thrown into the sarlacc's pit.

JABBA	Ahh!	
LEIA	—What role shall I play in this? I shall	70
	Not stand aside and let them fight for me.	
	I am no fragile damsel to be sav'd,	
	But have, since I was young, fought for myself.	

Thus, to my work: to slay the biggest foe—
Thou, Jabba, art for me and me alone!   75

FETT   I shall fly unto the fray, for no mere band of
rebels shall outwit the great Jabba of the Hutt.
They shall not easily defeat the one who doth
fill my coffers. Not, indeed, as long as Boba Fett
hath pow'r to live and breathe. To it!   80
                    [Lando fights with a guard and falls
                              off the skiff toward the pit.

LANDO   Alas, my friends, I fall!
                              [Boba Fett flies to the skiff.
                              Han Solo and Chewbacca fall.

LUKE   —Nay, thou vile Fett!
Thou shalt not have the best of us. A-ha!
                              [Luke strikes Boba Fett's blaster.
Thy blaster's now in twain by my lightsaber.

FETT   A hit, a very palpable hit! He hath torn my
blaster in twain with his lightsaber, but I shall   85
have him yet, and protect my great reward.
Go, ropes, and bind this rascal Jedi. Belike
Jabba shall further payment render when he
doth see the noble deeds done for his sake.
                    [Boba Fett binds Luke Skywalker with ropes,
                    but then is knocked down. Luke escapes and jumps
                              to another skiff, fighting the guards there.

LANDO   Han! Chewie! Can ye hear me?
HAN   —Lando!
CHEWBAC.   —Auugh!   90
                    [Boba Fett stands up and takes aim at Luke.

FETT   I have thee in my sights now, Jedi. Thou shalt
feel the pow'r of my rockets, and be no more.

CHEWBAC.   Egh!

HAN   —Boba Fett? What Boba Fett, and where?
              [Han Solo moves and activates Boba Fett's jets,
                      sending him flying into the pit.

FETT   Alas! The greatest Fett shall not die like this!
           O horrid Fate! Where is now my great reward?   95
              [Boba Fett falls into pit and dies.

JABBA   Nuh oola koobah!

LEIA   —Those shall be thy words
           Most final! Now, the chains that bind me to
           This wretched lump of flesh shall be my hope!
           Whilst Jabba worries o'er the battle, I
           Shall throw the chains about his neck. Then, pull!   100
           Aye, pull—a princess' vengeance! Die, thou brute!
           Thou unsuspecting Hutt, I curse thy life!
           For all the innocent whoe'er did die,
           For all the noble souls thou didst torment,

For all the gentle lives that are no more,   105
For all the galaxy's injustice—die!
    [Princess Leia strangles Jabba of the Hutt. He dies.

HAN   Good Lando, thou didst turn thy back on me,
But thou shalt have a chance to earn thy due
Since Luke and Chewie tell me of thy shame.
Chewbacca, lift me down that I may save   110
Him from a thousand years of pain.

LUKE   —Brave Han
Attempts to rescue Lando, but the gun
From on the barge doth block his progress. Fie!
No rest from trouble have we here—these foes
Will not let us escape without a fight.   115
They do intend to block us all the way—
Then to the barge, to aid the rescue. Fly!
            [Luke jumps onto Jabba's barge.

HAN   Pray, grasp the staff!

LANDO   —I almost have it!

CHEWBAC.   —Auugh!

LANDO   Alack! The sarlacc's tentacle wraps 'round
My leg. I fear this is the end! O give   120
Me strength to face my death well.

HAN   —Be thou still,
And Chewie, hand the blaster unto me.

LANDO   A blaster in the hands of one who's blind?
Methinks I may do better in the pit.
Good Han, think on the defects of thine eyes!   125

HAN   My sight is much improv'd: my aim is true!
          [Han Solo shoots the tentacle and
              lifts Lando onto the skiff.

LUKE   Good Lando is safe once again, and Han

And Chewie steady are upon the skiff.
Thus shall I find the droids and Leia, then
Destroy this barge and Jabba's courtiers all.   130

R2-D2   [*aside:*] Now to the princess, to release her bonds!

LEIA   All thanks, R2, now let us flee from here—
Find thou C-3PO, and we'll away!

R2-D2   Beep, squeak!

CRUMB   —My master's dead, but no fool I—
I'll fight these droids until my fate's secure.   135
         [*Salacious Crumb pokes at C-3PO's eyes.*

C-3PO   Mine eyes, alas—O R2, help!

R2-D2   —Meep, squeak!
              [*Aside:*] Tear not my friend apart, you tallow face!
                              [*R2-D2 shocks Salacious Crumb,*
                                        who jumps away.

CRUMB   The droid hath zapp'd me quite! O naughty imp!
C-3PO   O counterpart from Heaven sent, my thanks!
            But now, R2, say where dost thou lead me?   140
            Why do we swift approach the vessel's edge?
            This is most curious and passing strange,
            For I could not jump to the sand, and 'tis
            From here a mighty drop indeed—
                              [*R2-D2 pushes C-3PO off the edge of the*
                              barge into the sand and falls in after him.

R2-D2   —Nee, hoo!

LUKE   I prithee, Leia, take the gun and point   145
                It yonder, at the deck! The barge shall fall!
                          [Luke is shot in the hand by a guard.
                [*Aside:*] Alas, my hand, but 'tis my hand of steel,
                It causes me some pain, but not as 'twould
                Were it my own real flesh. Strange notion, this.
                I have not time to think on it, but shall,   150
                Another time, consider this my hand.

LEIA   The gun is pointed at the deck: 'tis time.

LUKE   Then let it fly, and we'll escape forsooth!
                'Tis well a rope is here to swing us o'er
                Another chasm—what serendipity!   155
                          [Luke and Princess Leia swing from the
                                    barge onto the skiff.

LEIA   [*aside:*] Once have I swung with him across a chasm,
                Now swing we once more to the waiting skiff.
                We have a way of swinging through our fears!

HAN   We all are now on board the skiff—away!
                This brave event shall be remember'd, Luke,   160
                And since I have been thaw'd, my warmest and
                My most sincere appreciation do
                I give thee for my rescue well devis'd.

LUKE   My friend, 'tis none but what thou wouldst for me.
                Now, let us flee—the droids, do not forget.   165

LANDO   We fly indeed, by foes no more beset.
                          [The barge explodes and all on board die.
                          Exeunt Luke Skywalker, Han Solo, Chewbacca,
                                    Princess Leia, Lando, R2-D2,
                                              and C-3PO on skiff.

SCENE 1.

Inside the second Death Star.

Enter CHORUS.

CHORUS The army of the Empire gathers near
Within the Death Star's uncompleted shell.
They all prepare to welcome one they fear:
The Emperor hath come, thereon to dwell.

[Exit chorus.

Enter EMPEROR PALPATINE *and* ATTENDING ROYAL GUARDS.

EMPEROR   My servant Vader have I come to meet,   5
           To hear him tell what progress hath been made
           Upon this newest Death Star. Confident
           I am that he shall make a good report,
           For he is ever trustworthy when ask'd
           To solve a problem for his Emperor.   10
           Forsooth, the man is all obedience
           When he is call'd to serve. It hath been so
           For years now, ever since he turn'd toward
           The dark side and became a Sith as I.
           But there is more than mere obedience: 15
           He looketh on me as a father, aye,
           For truly did I train him so to do.
           He doth respect and hang on ev'ry word
           I utter, even when 'tis to rebuke
           Or punish him for some apparent fault.   20
           The man is like a pet most pitiful,
           E'er braying for his master's notice and
           Displaying great affection e'en when kick'd.
           In truth, his groveling doth make me sick.
           Aye, his devotion to me I do not   25
           Reciprocate, for he to me is but
           A tool—most useful and most sharp, 'tis true—
           But merely agent of my will, no more.
           Yet he a vital purpose serveth in
           My reign and plans, while little doth he know   30
           That he could be more powerful than I.
           A tool the man may be, but I cannot
           Dispense with his keen services as yet.

But since I do consider him a threat,
I keep his leash as short as possible,   35
And I accept his childlike zeal for me
At least till I an apt replacement find.
Mayhap this young Skywalker—who is e'er
On Vader's otherwise clear mind—may prove
To be his aging father's substitute.   40
Was it a judgment error to inform
Darth Vader of the presence of his son?
Methinks 'twas not, for his devotion to
His Emperor and his submersion in
The dark side shall be more persuasive than   45
What feelings he may have for son unknown.
And furthermore, to know Skywalker is
His son shall heighten his resolve to turn
The boy unto the dark, and make him mine.
Thus would he see his Emperor and son   50
Together join'd, which would bring him dark joy.
'Tis surely how the future shall unfold—
All shall be well, for I have plann'd it so.
And now he comes: my humble servant Darth.

Enter DARTH VADER *and* MOFF JERJERROD *with* STORMTROOPERS.

VADER   I bid thee welcome and with humbl'd mien   55
             I bow to thee in utmost reverence:
             My master, teacher, savior, rescuer.
EMPEROR   Arise, my friend, and put thy soul at ease.
             I trust the time spent here shall bear good fruit?
VADER   Indeed, my master. All the workers have   60
             A newfound motivation for the task.

The Death Star shall completed be within
The time and schedule thou hast orderèd.
EMPEROR   Thou hast done well, Lord Vader. I am pleas'd.
And now I sense another thought in thee?   65
Thou wouldst anon resume thy search for the
Young rebel Skywalker. Have I judg'd right?
VADER   My master: yes.
EMPEROR   —Be patient, my good friend.
Thou shalt not seeker be; I'll warrant that,
In time, the lad himself shall seek thee out—   70
I see with my mind's eye it shall be so.
And when he doth come to thee, thou shalt then
Deliver him, in deference, to me.
The boy hath grown quite strong. Together we
Will bring him to the dark side of the Force.   75
VADER   Thy wish is mine.
EMPEROR   —Thus have we set the scene:
All doth proceed just as I have foreseen!

                                                    [Exeunt.

SCENE 2.

The Dagobah system.

Enter LUKE SKYWALKER *and* R2-D2, *speaking with* HAN SOLO
and PRINCESS LEIA *in comlink.*

LUKE   Good friends, with you I shall meet once again,
Where our strong fleet doth plan to rendezvous.
LEIA   [*through comlink:*] Aye, do. Th'Alliance should be
                                                    gather'd now.

HAN   [*through comlink:*] And Luke, my deepest thanks are
                                                          due to thee,
             For I did doubt that thou a Jedi wert.   5
             But thine example brave hath shown to me
             A power I ne'er would have believ'd was real,
             Except I was its benefici'ry.
             Thou didst not overlook thy friend in need,
             But came back for his rescue unafraid.   10
             Now truly, friend, 'tis I who owe thee one.
                            [*Exeunt Han Solo and Princess Leia.*

R2-D2   Beep, squeak, meep, beep, squeak, whistle,
                                                   whistle, meep?

LUKE   'Tis right, R2, we go to Dagobah—
             A promise must I keep to my old friend.
             [*Aside:*] This glove I place upon my injur'd hand,   15
             The hand that in the fight with Jabba was
             The sore recipient of blaster's touch.
             O hand, replete with wires and gears that move,
             With glove of black I cover the machine
             That lies within the skinlike covering,   20
             Which once a medic droid hath grafted on.
             How strange this hand, which feeleth like my flesh
             Yet is such stuff as droids are made of. Cold
             And dead, yet living, this is a device
             That serves me well but represents a dark   25
             And dismal fate. Aye, with this hand I have
             Become yet one step closer to the man
             Whose path I fear, yet wish to understand:
             Darth Vader, who my father claims to be.
             Indeed, I do believe his claim is true,   30
             But shall ask Yoda to confirm his words.

If he my father is, what shall it mean
For the Rebellion and for my own soul?
Shall my relations govern all my days,
Or may I yet escape mine origins?   35
Shall all the father's sins be visited
Upon the child, or shall I triumph yet?
Be with me, all ye Jedi past and gone—
I fly unto that place where first I learn'd
From Yoda, who is small, yet greater e'en   40
Than all my pow'rs or Master Obi-Wan.
With joy, I fly from here to see his face,
With hope, I fly to him to learn the truth,
With fear, I fly to him to know my path,
With expectation great, I fly to him.   45

Enter YODA.

Look now, he comes—alas, how ag'd he seems!
YODA   That face thou dost make:
        Look I so old to young eyes,
        My body so frail?
LUKE   Nay, nay, good master! Perish such a thought.   50
YODA   I do, aye, I do.
        Sick and weak have I become,
        Elderly and tir'd.

        And yet, I ask thee:
        When nine hundred years thou hast,   55
        Shalt thou look better?

        Soon shall I have rest,

Forever sleep, as all do.
Earnèd it I have.

LUKE   But what is this? Thou art an aging soul, 60
Yet wherefore speakest thou of death's embrace?
Good Master Yoda, cease: thou mayst not die.

YODA   Verily, 'tis true,
With the Force pow'rful am I,
Yet not that pow'rful. 65

Twilight is on me
And thence comes night. 'Tis the way
For all in the Force.

LUKE   Yet I have need of thy good help, for here
I stand, return'd, prepar'd my training to 70
Complete. What should I do without thine aid?

YODA   No further training
Dost thou require, for thou hast
All thou e'er shalt need.

LUKE   Forsooth, 'tis true: I am a Jedi now. 75

YODA   Be thou not so sure,
For still Vader remaineth.
Thou must confront him.

Then, and only then,
A true Jedi shalt thou be. 80
And face him thou shalt.

LUKE   Dear Master Yoda, one thing in me burns—
The question that is flame inside my bones,
Whose answer may yet kindle hate or love,
I know not which. Yet still it must be ask'd: 85
Darth Vader—tell me true—is he my father?

YODA	'Tis time for my rest.
	Time for my sleep eternal,
	'Tis no time for truth.
LUKE	Thou wouldst protect me from this knowledge,
	which 90
	May difficult and painful be. In this
	Thou showest care for me, and hast my thanks—
	But Yoda, full of heart, I must needs know.
YODA	[aside:] Alack, he knows all.
	Now may I only speak truth: 95
	Only truth lives on.
	[To Luke:] Thy father he is.
	Told you, did he? Unforeseen
	This is. Distressing.
LUKE	Distressing that at length I learn the truth? 100
YODA	Nay, nay! Distressing
	That thou hast rush'd to face him.
	Not ready wert thou.
	Thy training not done,
	The field of thy heart unplow'd, 105
	The burden, too much.
LUKE	Forgive me, for I knew not what I did.
YODA	Remember, my Luke,
	A Jedi's strength from the Force
	Doth come. But beware. 110
	Anger, fear, hatred—
	From the dark side they all come;
	Its minions they are.

Once thou hast enter'd
In the dark path infernal,   115
Abandon all hope.

The powers of the
Emperor, thou shouldst never
Underestimate.

Else thy father's fate,   120
Shall, in turn, become thine own:
Let not this transpire.

When I have gone, slept,
The last of the Jedi shalt
Thou be, thou alone.   125

Attend, Luke! The Force
Is strong with thy family:
Pass on what thou learn'dst.

These final words now
With my last breath I utter: 130
O hear well, brave Luke.

This is our hope: there
Is another Skywalker.
The rest silence is.

                                              [*Yoda dies.*

LUKE   Good night, sweet Jedi, noble, wise, and true.   135
              So gentle was he, and too quickly gone.
              O Fate, what hast thou brought into my life—

How shall I live when all I love have died?
Yet all things die, and all things pass away,
And all is like the sweeping of the stars   140
As one doth pass through lightspeed's rapid blaze.
We know 'tis true: no mortal does not know
That all are born to feed insatiate death.
But O, what grief we meet along the way:
The knowledge something beautiful is lost,   145
The deep regret for all unspoken words—
Profound remorse for healing never giv'n.
To wish to hold the dead one's hand again,
To picture a love's smile, and know it gone:
These are the pains that human life doth bring,   150
The heartache and the thousand nat'ral shocks
That flesh is heir to. Death shall not be tam'd,
It shall not lose its victory or sting,
Yet it shall never have the best of us
If in our living we have truly liv'd.   155
To love with bliss, to fight for righteousness,
To heed adventure's call, to cry with joy,
To laugh amidst life's greatest heights and depths:
This is the living that doth conquer death,
So e'en though it shall come, we shall not fear't.   160
These lessons let my master's death teach me,
That my life shall esteem his memory.

R2-D2   [*aside:*] O gift of Fate, that he my master is!
               [*To Luke:*] Beep, meep, beep, whistle, meep, beep,
                                        whistle, squeak!

LUKE   I cannot face the future by myself,   165
               What shall I do, R2? I am alone—
               The only Jedi left to bear the name.

It may be this responsibility
Is far too great for such a one as I.
How can I bear the burden by myself?   170

Enter GHOST OF OBI-WAN KENOBI.

OBI-WAN   Nay, not alone, for Yoda always shall
          Remain with thee.
LUKE   —My soul, 'tis Obi-Wan!
          [*Aside:*] Now e'en though he of ghostly matter's
                                                       made,
          He shall anon give answer for his words.
          [*To Obi-Wan:*] Good Ben, it warms my heart to
                                        see thee here,   175
          Yet I must ask thee to explain thyself—
          Pray, wherefore hast thou not reveal'd the thing
          That thou didst know? Thou said'st my father had
          By Vader been betray'd and murderèd.
          Ne'er hast thou said that he my father is!   180
OBI-WAN   [*aside:*] I never did imagine that, in death,
          I would be call'd upon to justify
          The words I spoke in life. 'Twas well I spoke
          Not of the midi-chlorians to Luke,
          For then he would have endless questions still.   185
          [*To Luke:*] Thine inquiry shall have an answer, Luke,
          For verily thou dost deserve to know.
          Thy father was seducèd by the dark
          Side of the Force. 'Twas then that he no more
          Was Anakin Skywalker, only Darth.   190
          When that had happen'd, thy good father was
          Destroy'd. And thus, forsooth, the words I spoke

	Were truthful, from a certain point of view.	
LUKE	"A certain point of view"? What doth that mean?	
	It may be said that I, within my ship,	195
	Do see my X-wing as an instrument	
	Of truth and justice, aye, a noble thing,	
	While from a certain point of view I know	
	Mine enemies do see it as a threat.	

LUKE   "A certain point of view"? What doth that mean?
It may be said that I, within my ship,   195
Do see my X-wing as an instrument
Of truth and justice, aye, a noble thing,
While from a certain point of view I know
Mine enemies do see it as a threat.
It may be said that when I was attack'd   200
By rancor vicious and intemperate,
Prepar'd to make of me his morning meal,
There is a certain point of view that doth
Suggest he was a simple hungry beast.
It may e'en be that our Rebellion is,   205
For us, an undertaking pure and good,
Possessing every virtue possible,
While from the Empire's certain point of view
It is a mere annoyance to be crush'd.
But this, I do not understand: how can   210
A certain point of view say that a man
Was murder'd by another man, when both
Are one and they together are my father?

OBI-WAN Luke, thou shalt find that many of your truths
Depend entirely on your point of view.   215
It well may be that thou dost like it not,
But does not follow that it is not so.
'Tis true, that Anakin a good friend was.
When I first knew him, he already was
A pilot skill'd and swift, and it amaz'd   220
Me with what strength the Force work'd in his life.
I took it on myself to train him as
A Jedi. Even then I did believe

	That I could train him just as Yoda could.	
	But there my fault did lie. Therein I fail'd.	225
LUKE	I do believe it may be rectified.	
	What if he could be turnèd once again?	
	There is yet good within him—I can feel't.	
OBI-WAN	He is machine e'en more than man, I fear.	
	His soul's an evil, tangl'd labyrinth.	230
LUKE	I shall not do it, Ben.	
OBI-WAN	—Thou canst not 'scape	
	Thy destiny. You must confront and face	
	Darth Vader once again.	
LUKE	—I shall not kill	
	My father.	
OBI-WAN	—Then the Emperor hath won.	
	Thou wert our only hope the Empire and	235
	The dark side to defeat. If thou wilt not,	
	No other shall arise to take our place.	
LUKE	But must this necessarily be so?	
	For Yoda spoke of yet another. Who?	
OBI-WAN	No more of hidden pasts: thou shalt know all.	240
	The other one of which he spoke is none	
	But thy twin sister.	
LUKE	—Sister? I know none.	
OBI-WAN	Both thou and she were hidden safely from	
	The Emperor just after ye were born.	
	For he did know, as I do, that the kin	245
	Of Anakin would be a pow'rful threat	
	Unto his reign of madness, might, and murder.	
	At birth, the two were separated: thou	
	Unto thine uncle Owen and thine aunt	
	Beru, on Tatooine, where I did watch	250

O'er thee as thou didst grow into a man;
Thy sister to a senator did go,
Apart from thee and thy dread father's wrath.
There she did grow into a woman fine,
And has, since then, remain'd anonymous.   255

LUKE [*aside:*] O wondrous revelation to my soul!
A sister, and before me comes her face:
For surely Leia is my sister, else
My instincts have no truth in them. What news!
I know not whether to respond with shouts   260
Of greatest joy, or to shrink back in fear
And paralyzing shock at what we've done.
Three times hath she kiss'd me in friendship's name,
The last of these more passionate than e'er
A sister should upon her sib bestow.   265
There is an ancient tale of Tatooine,
That tells of Tusken Raider who, through Fate
And circumstance, join'd with his mother in
A bond most strange and quite unnatural.
They liv'd in blissful ignorance of their   270
Relation until they discover'd it
By chance. And O, what awful times befell!
The Tusken Raider's mother hang'd herself
Upon a bantha's horn. The Tusken, in
His agony and grief, pull'd off his mask   275
And claw'd at his own eyes until they bled,
Then came dislodg'd, and finally pluck'd out.
He fell unto his knees and cried with pain—
Not merely pain to have his eyes remov'd,
But deeper pain that sear'd his very heart.   280
'Tis said that though he then could see no more,

He saw more clearly than he ever had.
At night, upon the sands of Tatooine,
His howl may still be heard, a warning to
Those who would break the sacred fam'ly bond   285
Through passions of the body. Shall this be
My fate, for crossing o'er the boundary
That none should cross, e'en once? I'll warrant: nay.
Not only have I superstitions none,
But our brief moments of affection were   290
A trifle none could call a love affair.
I now see clearly but still have my eyes,
And may my sister know sans tragedy.
Thus, I do make a solemn, earnest vow:
I shall embrace my royal sister as   295
A pow'rful ally, and shall show to her
The path that surely leads unto the Force.
[*To Obi-Wan:*] 'Tis Leia, aye? My soul doth know
                                     'tis she.

OBI-WAN   Thine instincts serve thee well, Luke. Bury now
These feelings, for they do thee credit but   300
May be manipulated and abus'd
If e'er the Emperor should learn of them.

LUKE   It bringeth my heart joy to see thee, Ben,
I'll heed thy counsel till we meet again.

                                   [Exeunt.

SCENE 3.

The rebel fleet, in space.

Enter HAN SOLO *and* LANDO OF CALRISSIAN.

HAN   My friend, well met! 'Tis good to see thee here
           And not a'dangling o'er a sarlacc's pit.
           Thou wast promoted well—a general!
LANDO   Belike our leaders were inform'd about
           Mine actions at the battle of Taanab.   5
HAN   Cast not thine eyes on me for blame or thanks—
           I did but tell them thou art pilot fair.
           But knew not that they hop'd to find the one
           Who would direct this crazy-brain'd attack.
LANDO   Nay, "crazy-brain'd" thou sayst? How may that be,   10
           Since thou dost know a thing or two of Death
           Star battles and what it doth take to win?
           Surpris'd I am that they did not ask thee.
HAN   But who hath said that they did not inquire?
           Yet I am not of madness made. And thou,   15
           Remember well, art fashion'd of respect.

Enter PRINCESS LEIA, CHEWBACCA, C-3PO, MON MOTHMA,
ADMIRAL ACKBAR, GENERAL MADINE, WEDGE ANTILLES,
and several REBEL PILOTS.

MOTHMA   I prithee, gather 'round, ye rebels all,
           And mark ye well the message I relay.
           The Emperor hath made a critical
           Mistake, and our time for attack is nigh.   20

The data brought to us by Bothan spies
Details th'exact location of the vast
New battle station that the Emperor
Hath underta'en to build. We also know
This battle station's weapon systems are   25
Not fully operational as yet.
Th'Imperi'l fleet is spread both far and wide
Throughout the galaxy, with hopes—quite vain—
That they shall soon engage us in a fight.
And while the fleet's away, the station hath   30
But minimal protection. This, my friends,
Would be good news enough, but there is more:
Reliable report hath come to us
That e'en the dreaded Emp'ror Palpatine
Himself doth oversee construction of   35
The Death Star, and is presently on board.
This news doth cheer us, friends, but pray recall
That many Bothans died to bring it here.
I call on Adm'ral Ackbar to unfold
Our plan so you may know your roles in this,   40
The final chapter of rebellion's tale.

       [Admiral Ackbar turns on a visual model of the
                Death Star and the forest moon of Endor.

ACKBAR   You may within this model see the Death
Star orbiting around the forest moon
Of Endor. Though the weapons systems on
The Death Star are not operational   45
As yet, the Death Star hath a strong defense:
It is secur'd by shield of energy
A'generated on the forest moon.
Deactivated must this shield be ere

	We can attack. Then, when the shield hath been	50
	Disarm'd, our cruisers shall take wing and fly	
	Within the superstructure to destroy	
	The main reactor. This attack shall be	
	Made by a squadron of our wingèd ships	
	Led by our General Calrissian,	55
	Who is a worthy and a noble chap.	
HAN	Good luck be thine, my friend. Thou shalt need it.	
ACKBAR	Thus endeth my report. Now General	
	Madine, thine efforts for our mission wilt	
	Thou presently recap?	
MADINE	—We've stolen an	60
	Imperi'l shuttle, which, disguisèd as	
	A cargo ship, shall use a secret code	
	To land upon the moon. Thereon a team	
	Shall fearlessly deactivate the shield.	
C-3PO	A dangerous experience, no doubt.	65
LEIA	[to Han:] And who, I wonder, has agreed to it?	
	For such a mission may quite futile prove.	
HAN	Nay, be thou not afraid. A man of wit,	
	Of clever mind and fine exterior	
	They must have chosen, whom thou shalt approve.	70
MADINE	Good Gen'ral Solo, is thy team prepar'd?	
LEIA	[aside:] A man of wit! He ne'er doth cease t'amaze.	
HAN	My team is ready, yet I do not have	
	A crew who shall the shuttle's flight command.	
CHEWBAC.	Auugh!	
HAN	—It shall not be easy, friend, thus I	75
	Had not yet volunteer'd thy worthy name.	
CHEWBAC.	Egh!	
HAN	—Well! Now have I one!	

LEIA   —And count me two.
                Good General, I gladly follow thee.
                Wherever thou dost go, then so shall I,
                Wherever thou remain, thus I shall too,   80
                Thy people shall my people be as well,
                And all thy battles shall my battles be.

                    Enter LUKE SKYWALKER *and* R2-D2.

LUKE   Why have but two when three is company?
                I shall go with thee also, noble friend.
                [*Aside:*] My sister! Ah! To see her fills my heart!   85
                        [*Luke Skywalker and Princess Leia embrace.*
LEIA   What is't?
LUKE   —Ask yet again, another time.
HAN   Ho, Luke!
LUKE   —Good Han, and Chewie!
R2-D2   —Beep, meep, squeak!
C-3PO   "Exciting" would not be my word of choice,
                'Tis more like "harrowing," if I were ask'd.
                                [*Exeunt all but Han Solo and
                                    Lando of Calrissian.*
HAN   Now preparation's made, good Lando, yet   90
                A word with thee ere thou depart, my friend:
                With heart sincere I proffer this to thee:
                Take thou my ship, the brave *Millenn'um Falcon*.
                Thou shalt be greatly aided in thy task
                If thou wilt take the fastest ship that e'er   95
                Did fly within our galaxy. Thou dost
                Have more experience with this swift ship
                Than any but Chewbacca and myself.

Thou art a skill'd and worthy pilot, and
I trust that thou shalt keep her safe.

LANDO   —'Tis well,   100
I am persuaded, and shall take the ship
And leave with thee both gratitude and my
Assurance that I know how deeply thy
Heart stirs for her. Thus do I pledge: I shall
Take care of her as though she were my own,   105
And shall deliver her sans e'en a scratch.

HAN   [*aside:*] This Lando doth protest too much, methinks.
I was not nervous till he made his pledge.
[*To Lando:*] No scratch, indeed. I take with me thy
                                                      word.

LANDO   We part, thou pirate true. And Han, good luck.   110
HAN   To thee as well, good friend.

                    [*Exit Lando of Calrissian as Han Solo
                    boards the Imperial shuttle* Tydirium.

        Enter LUKE SKYWALKER, CHEWBACCA, C-3PO, *and*
            R2-D2 *in the cockpit with Han Solo.*

CHEWBAC.   —Auugh.
HAN   —Nay, I think
The Empire had not Wookiees on their minds
When they design'd her, Chewie. Are we set?

                Enter PRINCESS LEIA.

I see the good *Millenn'um Falcon* yon,
And wonder how the die for her is cast.   115
LEIA   Art thou awake, or dost thou slumber on?

HAN	A feeling tells me this look is my last.
CHEWBAC.	Auugh.
LEIA	—General, let us depart.
HAN	—Aye, true—

Now let's see what this heap of junk can do!
   [Exeunt, flying off in the shuttle Tydirium.

SCENE 4.

Inside the second Death Star.

Enter DARTH VADER.

VADER The strangest feelings have been mine of late.
To know my son exists confounds my wits
As I did ne'er imagine. What is this
Confusion that doth obfuscate my mind?
For evil I am made, for punishment   5
Of foes, for conquering of peoples, and
To do the perfect will of my great lord
And Emperor. Of these I certain am,
For this hath been my role full many years.
Yet where within this surety is room   10
For offspring? For a son? What can a life
Liv'd on the dark side of the Force have still
To do with heirs, with flesh and bone that sprang
From me and that sweet life that once I led?
How can this Sith, this man of pain and death, 15
Be father to the fruit of far-gone love?
It seems well nigh impossible when one
Considers what I've been. For, verily,

I may not hide the man I truly am:
A warrior devoted to the cause   20
Of Emperor and Empire both. 'Tis who
I am: I must be mad when I have cause
And smile at no one's jests. No humor doth
Give pleasure to my mouth or stir my heart,
Nor would I dare to ever love again,   25
If e'en this mess of tangl'd wires could love.
I am a Sith, most surely to be fear'd.
Yet that perplexing thing remains: a son.

Enter EMPEROR PALPATINE *and* ROYAL GUARDS.

What is thy bidding, master?
EMPEROR   —Send the fleet
Unto the farthest side of Endor. There   30
Let it remain, until 'tis callèd for.
VADER   What of the recent news that rebels are
Amassing near to Sullust? Is it so?
EMPEROR   It is of little consequence, for soon
This vile Rebellion shall be crushèd and   35
Young Skywalker shall know the dark side's pow'r.
Thy work upon the Death Star is complete.
Thou shalt go hence to the command ship, and
Await my orders there.
VADER   —My master: aye.
                                [Exit Darth Vader.
EMPEROR   Now all the players and the scenes are set   40
To bring about our greatest triumph yet.
                                        [Exeunt.

ACT III

SCENE 1.

On the Imperial shuttle Tydirium *and the Super Star Destroyer.*

Enter Luke Skywalker, Han Solo, Chewbacca, Princess Leia,
C-3PO, *and* R2-D2. *Enter* Admiral Piett *and* Imperial
controller *on balcony, on the Super Star Destroyer.*

HAN   Now if the Empire is not by our ruse
                Deceiv'd, we must fly quickly, Chewie.
CHEWBAC.   —Auugh.
CONTROL.   We have you on our screens; identify
                Yourselves.
HAN   —The shuttle of *Tydirium*
                Requests deactivation of the shield   5
                Of energy.
CONTROL.   —*Tydirium*, transmit
                Your clearance code for passage through the shield.
HAN   Transmission doth commence.
LEIA   —Now shall we learn
                If all these codes were worth the price we paid
                For them—the loss of friends, the loss of life.   10
HAN   Aye, it shall work, 'twas sacrifice well made.
CHEWBAC.   Egh!
LUKE   —Vader is aboard that giant ship.
HAN   Be not afear'd, good Luke, let not thy nerves
                Thy better judgment mar. Full many ships
                There are that do command the Empire's fleet.   15
                Keep thou thy distance, though, Chewbacca, but
                Do not appear as though thou keepest it.

CHEWBAC.   Auugh?

HAN   —Let me make it plain: fly casual.

CHEWBAC.   Egh!

          Enter DARTH VADER *on balcony.*

VADER   —Tell me now: where is that shuttle bound?

PIETT   Small shuttle of *Tydirium*, what is   20
           Thy destination and thy cargo? Speak!

HAN   We come to bring both parts and crew, which shall
           Deliver technical assistance to
           Our comrades on the forest moon.

VADER   —Have they
           The code that clearance would ensure?

PIETT   —They do.   25
           It is an older code, but hits the mark.
           I was about to grant them passage, Lord.

LUKE   [*aside:*] My father, how I sense him clearly now!
           His thoughts, his aspect, e'en his very mood.
           [*To Han Solo:*] I have endangerèd the mission here,   30
           And should not hither have accomp'nied you.

HAN   'Tis thine imagination, Luke. Pray, be
           More optimistic; let thy heart be still.

LUKE   [*aside:*] What stillness can there be when moves the
                               Force?
           It shall move mountains if it so desires.   35
           No inner strength or outer brawn can match
           The movement of the Force that now 'twixt me
           And Vader passeth. Han hath no idea,
           Yet all, belike, shall know quite soon enough,
           For Ben and Yoda both were right: I must   40

My father yet confront ere I—or he—
Shall ever freedom know.
PIETT   [*to Vader:*]   —Shall they be held?
VADER   Nay, Admiral, thou mayst let them proceed.
They shall be mine—mere cards that I shall play,
And I shall serve as dealer for their deck.   45
PIETT   Then shall I wager that the house shall win.
Thy wish is mine, my Lord, and it shall be.
[*To controller:*] Thou canst now carry on, and let
them pass.

HAN   This hesitation pregnant is with doubt:
Mayhap they are not taken in, Chewbacca.   50
CONTROL.   Good shuttle of *Tydirium*, the swift
Deactivation of the shield begins.
Hold fast unto thy present course.
                    [*Exeunt Darth Vader, Admiral Piett,*
                         and Imperial controller.
HAN   —'Tis well!
Did I not tell ye all that it would work?
No problems here, when Han is at the helm.   55
LEIA   My scoundrel-love, thou ever hast a boast—
Yet often there's a reason to thy rhyme.

Enter several IMPERIAL SCOUTS, *aside, as*
Luke Skywalker, Han Solo, Chewbacca,
Princess Leia, C-3PO, and R2-D2 disembark.

HAN   Now have we landed on the forest moon,
And our good company has disembark'd.
We make our way through trees and bushes here.   60
But what is that, a sound—pray all, alert!

C-3PO   You see, R2, I told thee this would be
             Quite dangerous. Alack, be calm, my core!
HAN   I see a building with Imperial
             Motifs and markings. There, beside it, are   65
             Two scouts. This shall require some care, methinks.
LEIA   Then shall we try and go around the side?
LUKE   It will take time.
HAN   —And all shall be for naught
             If we are seen. Yet I do have a plan:
             Chewbacca and myself shall handle this.   70
             Ye both stay here.
LUKE   —But prithee, soft, good Han.
             Be quiet, for there may be others near.
HAN   Thy words unnecessary are—'tis me!
                         *[Han Solo and Chewbacca move
                                  toward the Imperial scouts.*
             Now shall I move in stealth to take them in,
             Then take them out. With catlike tread I step,   75
             Ne'er to be notic'd till my prey is mine,
             Then I—alack! A twig snaps underfoot!
                         *[Imperial Scouts 1 and 2 turn toward the sound
                                  and see Han Solo and Chewbacca.*
SCOUT 1   What is that sound? Alas, 'tis rebels, go!
             And warn our comrades quickly.
LUKE   —Let us fly!
                         *[Han fights with Imperial Scout 1.
                         Imperial Scout 2 boards his speeder bike
                                  to fly away but is shot by Chewbacca.
                                  Imperial Scouts 3 and 4 jump on
                                  their speeder bikes and fly away.*
LEIA   Behold the two scouts speed from out our grasp!   80

Upon the instant I shall give them chase.

LUKE   Pray, Leia, patience—straight I come with thee!
[Luke and Leia board a speeder bike behind
Imperial Scouts 3 and 4, in pursuit. Exeunt
Han Solo, Chewbacca, C-3PO, and
R2-D2 in the melee.

Enter CHORUS.

CHORUS   Do not our play too harshly judge, dear friends,
For with imagination may you see:
Into the forest now the fight extends   85
On speeder bikes that whip 'twixt tree and tree.
What haste their dauntless riders undergo
As they fly swiftly past both brush and stumps!
The rapid derring-do our scene doth show,
And when 'tis over, some shall have their lumps.   90
[Exit chorus.

LUKE   Jam thou their comlink, center switch!
LEIA   —'Tis done!
LUKE   Canst thou yet closer go? Pray, pull aside
The one before us. Now I jump aboard
His bike, and he is mine and I'm for him.
[Luke throws Imperial Scout 3 from his
speeder bike, and Imperial Scout 3 dies.

Enter IMPERIAL SCOUTS 5 *and* 6 *on speeder bikes.*

Aye, he is gone, but others take his place!   95
Good Leia, follow that one up ahead.
I shall remain behind, to face these two.

LEIA   'Tis well. Be safe, and I shall see thee soon.

LUKE   [*aside:*] O sister, all my thanks for tender words.

> *[Luke falls behind, alongside*
> *Imperial Scouts 5 and 6.*

Now shall this bike's keen blaster find its mark!   100
I shoot, and one is dead; the other next.

> *[Luke shoots and kills Imperial Scout 6.*

LEIA   I shall fly high o'er this one's bike, that he
May think that I have fled. Then shall I from
Above make my attack. Ha! Now beside
His bike, surprise is my sure strategy.   105

> *[Imperial Scout 4 shoots at Leia.*

Alas! My bike is hit, and off I fall!

> *[Leia falls to the ground, unconscious.*
> *Imperial Scout 4 looks behind him*
> *to make sure she has fallen.*

SCOUT 4	Ha! There's a rebel scum who shall no more
	Make trouble for our mighty Empire. We
	Are e'er the strongest in the galaxy,
	With pilots such as I whose skill is—O!— 110
	[Imperial Scout 4 collides with a tree and dies.
LUKE	This latest scout is skill'd beyond the rest—
	I may not best him in a battle thus.
	Yet by another method I shall win,
	For why rely on bikes and blasters when
	I have the Force, and my lightsaber, too? 115
	[Luke leaps from his bike.
	Now to it, scout! Return and meet thy fate!
	He comes a'blasting, but my lightsaber
	Deflects the shots, and now I slice his bike!
	Aye, broke in twain his bike doth falter fast,
	And now against a tree he meets his end! 120
	[Imperial Scout 5 dies.

Enter HAN SOLO, CHEWBACCA, C-3PO,
and R2-D2, *from the opposite side.*

R2-D2	Beep, meep, beep, whistle, meep, squeak, whistle, nee!
C-3PO	O, Gen'ral Solo, someone comes anon!
HAN	*[seeing Luke:]* Luke! We have found thee! But thou
	lack'st one thing:
	I bid thee tell me: where is Leia? Eh?
LUKE	She came not back?
HAN	—I thought she was with thee. 125
LUKE	And truly was. But lo, within the wood,
	The battle was borne out with speed and fire,
	Amid the blasts and cruel Imperi'l scouts

'Twas only muddledom that won the day.
We separated were, and there's an end.   130
Anon! We must fly hence and search for her.
Good R2, come, thy scanners we shall need.

C-3PO   Fear not, good master, we know what to do!
[*To R2-D2:*] And thou didst say 'twas pretty here. O pish!

            [*Exeunt Luke Skywalker, Han Solo,*
                 Chewbacca, C-3PO, and R2-D2.

Enter WICKET, *an Ewok, approaching Princess Leia.*

WICKET   A buki buki,   135
           Luki, luki,
           Issa creecher,
           Nuki, nuki!

            [*Wicket jabs Princess Leia with*
                 his staff. She wakes up.

LEIA   Desist at once, thou furry little imp!
WICKET   E danvay, danvay,   140
           Staa awanvay,
           Da livvy creecher!
           Panvay, panvay!
LEIA   I shall not hurt thee, little one. But O,
       My body cries with soreness from my fall.   145
       I wonder where Luke and the others are?
WICKET   Fangowa, gowa,
           I nonowa.
           Da creecher muvvee
           Slowa, slowa.   150
LEIA   It seemeth I am fix'd and grounded here,
       Yet I am lost and know not what "here" means.

All that I have is this small creature, from
A species I have ne'er encounterèd.
Mayhap thou wilt assist me, little friend.   155
Sit down beside me, here, and let us talk.
I promise I'll not hurt thee. Aye, approach.

WICKET   A dunga, dunga,
          Wassee wunga?
          Ino commee,   160
          Junga junga.

LEIA   Belike thou wouldst like something thou canst eat?
          If thou art like most creatures, thou mayst be
          Directed by thy stomach's wish for food—
          Where bellies lead, the other members trail.   165
          Here, friend, taste thou this morsel from my hand.

WICKET   Aytru, aytru,
          See mebbe tru,
          Iya tryee,
          Maytru, maytru.   170

                            [Wicket takes a wafer from
                             Princess Leia and eats it.

LEIA   I'll warrant I have made a friend at last—
          The food succeeds where words alone have fail'd.
          Now shall I take this helmet off, for sure,
          It gives me pain to wear it still so tight.

WICKET   A kusha kusha,   175
          Wassee doona?
          Mia scardu,
          Pusha, pusha.

LEIA   Nay, fear thou not, O little one; 'tis but
          A hat, and shall not harm thee. 'Tis no threat.   180
          Thou art a scamp fill'd full of skittishness.

                    [Wicket hears a sound in the forest.

WICKET   A kiata, ata,
                Summink mata,
                Summink commee,
                Giata ata.   185

                    [A shot is fired near Princess Leia,
                           who falls to the ground.

LEIA   *[aside:]* This creature's customs and his language are
                Unknown to me, and yet his instincts prove
                Most capable. He smell'd the danger ere
                I knew 'twas here. A pow'rful ally might
                He and his people be, if e'er we could   190
                Communicate and share each other's thoughts
                And hopes and aspirations openly.

                             [Another shot is fired.

WICKET   A wundah wundah,
                Shutee gundah,
                Shutee baddee,   195
                Nundah nundah.

                             [Wicket hides.

         Enter IMPERIAL SCOUTS 7 *and* 8.

SCOUT 7   *[to Leia:]* Stand down, milady, else you breathe your last!
                [To Scout 8:] Go, get thy bike, and take her back to base,
                For none but our own troops have clearance to
                Be on the sanctuary moon. She must   200
                Give answer for her furtive presence here.
SCOUT 8   Indeed, Sir.

                    [Imperial Scout 8 begins to exit. Wicket comes
                       out of hiding and strikes Imperial Scout 7.

SCOUT 7   —O! What manner of a beast—
                        [*Princess Leia hits Imperial Scout 7, who falls*
                            unconscious. Imperial Scout 8 begins to run.

LEIA   Now, blaster, hit thy mark, else we're found out!
                        [*Princess Leia shoots and kills Imperial Scout 8.*
                  Good cheer! The scout is slain, and we are safe.
                  I give thee thanks, thou bantam warrior,   205
                  For thy protection and thy bravery.
                  Come, let us go at once, ere others come.

WICKET   A yubnub, yubnub,
                  Shessa noolub,
                  Shessa frenda,   210
                  Yubyub, yubyub.

LEIA   [*aside:*] Although it seems I came from over there
                  He wisheth me to follow him that way.
                  Belike in following I'll earn his trust.
                  Then shall I make our budding friendship real   215
                  And see what this chance meeting may reveal.
                                                            [*Exeunt.*

SCENE 2.
Inside the second Death Star.

Enter DARTH VADER, EMPEROR PALPATINE,
and ROYAL GUARDS.

EMPEROR   Now wherefore hast thou come to see me here?
                  Thine orders were to stay aboard thy ship.

VADER   I would not disobey thine orders, were
                  It not of grave importance to our cause.

	A rebel force hath made it past the shield,	5
	And landed on the forest moon of Endor.	
EMPEROR	I know all this already.	
VADER	—And my son	
	Is with them on their mission.	
EMPEROR	—Art thou sure?	
VADER	Forsooth, for I have felt him.	
EMPEROR	—Strange that I	
	Have not. Lord Vader, are thy feelings on	10
	This matter clear, or need'st thou clarity?	
VADER	[*aside:*] Well ask'd, for my confusion he doth sense.	
	[*To Emperor:*] My thoughts are clear, my master.	
EMPEROR	—This, then, shalt	
	Thou do: fly to the sanctuary moon,	
	And wait upon him there, for he shall come.	15
VADER	Indeed? 'Tis he who shall come unto me?	
EMPEROR	I have foreseen it. His compassion for	
	His long-lost father shall mean his defeat.	
	'Tis he shall come to thee, and thou shalt bring	
	Him hither, unto me. Thus it shall be.	20
VADER	Whatever thou dost wish, I grant to thee.	

                                                              [*Exeunt.*

SCENE 3.

The forest moon of Endor.

Enter Han Solo, Chewbacca,
C-3PO, *and* R2-D2.

HAN   A'searching in the forest, we have found
                 No trace of my belovèd. Yet I see
                 These wreck'd and tangl'd bikes afore mine eyes,
                 And must assume the worst. Some horrid fate,
                 Some accident of fortune hath befall'n,   5
                 And ta'en my love too quickly from my grasp.
                 O let it ne'er be so, and let me not
                 With grief and anguish live out all my days.
                 Although we find not Leia, let us still
                 Some hope discover deep within these woods.   10

Enter Luke Skywalker, *holding Princess Leia's helmet.*

LUKE   This helmet have I found, near yonder log.
                 The tree that once so tall and stately stood,
                 Hath been by some unnat'ral force knock'd down.
                 But all that doth remain there is the top,
                 That once rose high above the forest's roof.   15
                 O tree, that lost its trunk and turn'd to log!
                 O helmet—without wearer—turn'd to shell.
C-3PO   Good Master Luke, his heart doth break within.
LUKE   Two more wreck'd speeders yonder did I see,
                 And this poor, empty helmet tells a tale.   20
C-3PO   I fear that R2's sensors can find no

	Suggestion of dear Princess Leia near.
HAN	I hope—O greatest hope, O fondest hope—
	With all my being hope she may be well.
CHEWBAC.	Auugh!
HAN	—What is it, thou Wookiee?

> [Chewbacca finds a piece of meat
> hanging from a rope.

CHEWBAC.	—Egh. Egh, auugh!	25
HAN	I do not understand, Chewbacca. It
	Is just a piece of meat, and nothing more.
CHEWBAC.	Auugh!
LUKE	—Nay! Pray, patience!

> [All are caught in a net and raised into the air.

HAN	—Wonderful! The ones
	Who wish'd to find become the ones found out,
	Who wish'd to net a princess, netted are,	30
	Who pray'd to find her, find themselves now prey.
	And why? Because the one who thinketh least
	Hath thought with appetite and not with mind.
LUKE	Since fault of thought hath got us to this place,
	Let us be calm, and reason our way out.	35
	Canst thou reach my lightsaber, Han?
HAN	—Indeed!

> [Han Solo tries but cannot reach the lightsaber.

R2-D2	[aside:] Once more it lies in me to save these men.
	Mayhap a fall upon their rears shall serve
	Them well. Now quickly to thy work, my blade!

> [R2-D2 begins to cut the net.

C-3PO	R2, dost think that wise? 'Tis far to fall!	40
LUKE	Down, down, we fall!
HAN	—Alack!

C-3PO   —O, R2!
CHEWBAC.   —Auugh!
HAN   Safe from the net, yet hard upon the ground.
             Although my mind is grateful for the help,
             My back doth cry for vengeance on the droid
             Whose foolish act hath knock'd us flat.

Enter EWOKS, *including* TEEBO, *surrounding the others.*

LUKE   —But look,   45
             How many furry beings are there here!
             O brave new world, that has such creatures in't!
                         [*Teebo points his spear at Han Solo.*
TEEBO   U jabbeh, jabbeh,
             Ussah stabbatheh,
             Unoh muvva,   50
             Gabbeh, gabbeh.
HAN   Avaunt, thou scruffy flea-infested imp—
             Point not thy spear toward my angry self,
             Else thou shalt know the scourge of blaster fire.
LUKE   I prithee, patience, Han—all shall be well.   55
TEEBO   E hura hura,
             Heeno scura,
             Heesa tempurr,
             Gura, gura.
LUKE   Chewbacca, give thy crossbow unto them.   60
             Let them believe they have the upper hand,
             And we shall see of what the beasts are made.
C-3PO   [*rising from the fall:*] Alas, my head! What pains I
                                        must endure.
             But O—what creatures do surround us here?

TEEBO	U hadoo, hadoo,	65
	Heesa gadoo,	
	Heesa mytee,	
	Gadoo, gadoo.	
C-3PO	A treeto treeto,	
	Meesah greeto,	70
	Houdi dootee,	
	Seeto, seeto.	
LUKE	C-3PO, dost comprehend their tongue?	
C-3PO	Indeed, my master Luke! Recall that I	
	Am fluent in more than six million forms—	75
HAN	Less prating, more explaining, droid. What didst	
	Thou say to them, when thou didst speak e'en now?	
C-3PO	"Hello," methinks. 'Tis possible I am	
	Mistaken. They employ a primitive	
	And ancient dialect, but it appears	80
	They think of me as like unto a god.	
R2-D2	[aside:] O heaven help us all. C-3PO	
	Already thinks himself divine, and needs	
	No congregation further. [To C-3PO:] Beep, squeak!	
CHEWBAC.	—Auugh!	
HAN	O Lord most high and reverent, thou gold	85
	And stainless deity, call on thy pow'rs	
	And godlike charms, and straight divine us all	
	A way beyond this situation. Aye?	
C-3PO	Nay, Gen'ral Solo, 'tis not proper.	
HAN	—Proper?	
	You shall for sure discover what is right	90
	And proper, when I blast apart thy frame.	
C-3PO	Lo, 'tis forbidden, Gen'ral Solo, for	
	E'en droids aren't masters of divinity.	

HAN   Thou fickle spirit! Deity or not,
             I shall a spiritual experience   95
             Enjoy as I do tear thee limb from limb.
                              [The Ewoks surround and
                                     threaten Han Solo.

TEEBO   Na goo, na goo,
             Heesall na doo,
             Heesall beest ill,
             Ya doo, ya doo.   100

HAN   Pray pardon, jolly beasts. Nay, fear me not—
             'Twas but a jest, for he is my old friend.
                       [The Ewoks bind Luke Skywalker, Han Solo,
                              Chewbacca, and R2-D2 and take them to
                                     their village, with C-3PO enthroned.

LUKE   Now are we ta'en unto their simple homes—
             Plain huts of wood with branches for their roofs.
             A simple tribe are these, yet wise as well—   105
             With neither guns nor lightsabers they snar'd
             A pilot skill'd, a Wookiee brave and strong,
             A Jedi Knight, and two most earnest droids.
             'Twas quite a catch for such a humble net.
             And now, like spits upon a fire we're hung.   110
             But what transpireth next? We'll see anon.

HAN   My feelings are o'ercome with thoughts most dire:
             They ready for a feast, but where's the food?
             Do they not know I shall a poor meal make?
             No supper may be cook'd from Han's firm flesh,   115
             For smuggler meat is all too hard and tough.

CHEWBAC.   Auugh!

TEEBO   E krandeh krandeh,
             Thessah mandeh,

	Thessah kuukah,	
	Gandeh, gandeh,	120
C-3PO	Ad toyum toyum,	
	Lessum goyum,	
	Nossah dootis,	
	Noyum, noyum.	

C-3PO   Thessah kuukah,
        Gandeh, gandeh,   120
        Ad toyum toyum,
        Lessum goyum,
        Nossah dootis,
        Noyum, noyum.

HAN   —Prithee, tell me, droid, what did he say?   125

C-3PO   O, it is rather an embarrassment
        Good Gen'ral Solo. It appears that thou
        Shalt be the main course at a banquet in
        My honor. I am quite asham'd, good Sir,
        And promise I shall not enjoy the meal.   130

CHEWBAC.   Auugh!

[Ewoks begin playing drums.

EWOKS   *[singing:]* A gunda gunda,
        Thissa funda,
        Thessa burna,
        Kunda, kunda.

Enter PRINCESS LEIA.

LUKE   —Leia!

HAN   —O, my heart! My precious one!   135
        My Leia! Now may I go up in flames,
        Since I have seen thee safe and well again,
        Belovèd.

C-3PO   —Royal Highness!

LEIA   —What is this
        That doth transpire here? Luke and Han bound up?

[Leia approaches but is stopped by Ewoks.
[To Ewoks:] Nay, do not hinder me, my newfound

friends. 140

	These goodly men are dear to me, they are

These goodly men are dear to me, they are
The closest that I have to family.
Pray, still your doubtful, cautious minds, and I
Shall show ye that these people mean no harm.
C-3PO, thou somehow art enthron'd,   145
Which doth suggest thou hast some sway o'er them.
Serve thou as translator, and tell these imps
To free our brave companions from their bonds.

C-3PO   [*to Teebo:*] I rooktah rooktah,
          Nowyee looktah,   150
          Lessem freeum,
          Booktah, booktah.
               [*The Ewoks continue their preparations for the feast.*

HAN   It seemeth that thy kingly words did fall
          Upon their peasant ears a little less
          Than royally.

LUKE   —Good 3PO, relay   155
          To them that if they shall not heed thy words,
          Thou wilt astound them with thine anger fierce,
          And ply thy magic on them.

C-3PO   —Magic, Sir?
          I know not what you mean. I have no magic!

LUKE   I prithee: argue not, but tell them now.   160

C-3PO   [*to Ewoks:*] No gosh, no gosh,
          I yami bosh,
          I uzzee prahnkh,
          E boomabosh.
               [*The Ewoks stop momentarily and
                    then resume their preparations.*

          O, see'st thou, Master Luke? They paid no heed,   165

As I suspected they would not, the brutes!

LUKE   [*aside:*] Now Force, come flow within, around, above.

Raise up the droid upon his wooden throne,

And let these creatures think he is their god,

A'raging in his anger. Let them shrink   170

And cower in their fear, and be so mov'd

That they shall do his every command.

C-3PO lifts up above the ground

And is quite terrified to be so high.

But frighten'd as they are, they do not see   175

Their god is yet more petrified than they.

They scatter to and fro and up and down,

For here's a sight they ne'er have seen before:

A being flying sans the use of wings.

O work thy power, Force, be thou my aid   180

And constant strong companion in our need.

Success! The creatures now are quite convinc'd,

And move with haste to free us of our bounds.

C-3PO doth lower into place,

And now we all are free—O thank the Force,   185

That mov'd in me so I could move the droid,

And move these creatures to release us all.

> [*The Ewoks unbind Luke Skywalker, Han Solo, and*
> *Chewbacca. An Ewok frees R2-D2 and R2-D2*
> *shocks the Ewok. The Ewok runs away.*

R2-D2   [*aside:*] Now come ye back, ye scurvy, furry things,

I'll shock ye all for your abuse of us.

HAN   O mistress mine, to see thee brings me joy!   190

Draw nigh and plant upon my lips a kiss.

LEIA   Luke hath secur'd your safety with his ploy—

No sweeter meeting can I wish than this!

                                        [*Han Solo and Princess Leia kiss.*
                                          Wicket approaches R2-D2.

WICKET   W'goodo, goodo,
              Whoosah yoodo,   195
              Yoosah speccul,
              Hoodo, hoodo.

LUKE   [*to C-3PO:*] My gratitude profound, C-3PO.

C-3PO   Forsooth, I never knew 'twas in me, Sir.

LUKE   These little creatures may have value yet   200
              If they our allies in this fight become.
              I need thine aid now to convince them so—
              I prithee, 3PO, make known to them
              Our dire adventures 'gainst the Empire vile.

C-3PO   I know not, Master. I am not a bard   205
              Who can with skillful tongue his story tell.

LEIA   But try, C-3PO—the tale relay
              In their own language.

                                        [*The Ewoks gather and listen.*

C-3PO   —All the world's at war,
              And all the rebels in it are the heroes;
              They have their battles and their skirmishes,   210
              And rebels in these scenes have play'd their parts,
              Their story being seven ages. First,
              Our princess that was captur'd was then sav'd,
              But Alderaan did pay the costly price.
              And then the Death Star battle, with its guns   215
              And awful loss of life, like speeder bikes
              We flew unto the final vict'ry. Then
              To Hoth, so barren, with a woeful ballad
              Compos'd for our lost comrades. Then to Bespin,
              Full of strange imps and fearful twists of fate.   220

My master fac'd Darth Vader, quick in quarrel,
While Lando, Chewie, and the princess just
Escap'd the cannon's mouth. But then our Han—
In fair trim belly with good humor lin'd,
With eyes severe and hair of scruffy cut,   225
Full of harsh tongue and modern instances—
Was plac'd in carbonite. The sixth age shift'd
To Tatooine, a lean and lonely place,
With Jabba there to give us all a fright.
The sarlacc vicious was a world too wide   230
For us to spend eternity within.
We turn'd again to Master Luke, who with
The Force did save our lives. Last scene of all,
That ends this brave eventful history,
Shall be the Empire's fall t'oblivion,   235
Sans pow'r, sans hate, sans fear, sans ev'rything.
                          [The Ewoks discuss the story.

HAN   What do they say?
LEIA   —I do not know.
LUKE   [*aside:*]   —I sense
     The keen nobility within their hearts;
     These small but mighty creatures shall yet be
     Our help as we make battle 'gainst our foes.   240
TEEBO   Na doonga doonga,
     Tymee soonga,
     Weesa hilpuh,
     Loonga, loonga.
C-3PO   'Tis wonderful! A sign of deep respect   245
     The group has given us, for we have been
     Made members of their honorable tribe.
     Moreover, they shall aid us in the fight

Against the Empire and its bunker here.

[*All embrace, and an Ewok hugs Han Solo.*

HAN   'Tis verily a dream come true for me.   250

[*Aside:*] And now, unhand me, teddy, ere I scream.

R2-D2   Beep, whistle, squeak!

LUKE   [*aside:*]   —This joyous scene doth stir

My soul, for since my presence here is but

A danger to my friends, I must depart.

[*Exit Luke Skywalker.*

LEIA   But wherefore doth Luke flee when we should all   255

Be celebrating? I shall follow him.

[*Exit Princess Leia.*

CHEWBAC.   Egh.

HAN   —So the proverb says, Chewbacca: "Help

That is but short is better than no help

At all." Though how the furry beasts will help

I cannot yet imagine or conceive.   260

C-3PO   The Ewok chief reports the scouts shall show

Us to the place that generates the shield

For the new Death Star. There we may fulfill

Our plan: deactivate the shield anon.

HAN   Well done, C-3PO, now quickly heed   265

Mine every command: first have them tell

Us how far distant is the place. Then be

Thou sure that, second, thou dost ask for fresh

Supplies. And fin'lly, get our weapons back.

But wherefore dost thou wait, thou simple droid?   270

Unto my tasks—I shall not wait for thee!

[*Exeunt Han Solo and Chewbacca.*

C-3PO   He cannot wait, but will not let me do't!

[*Exeunt.*

Enter LUKE SKYWALKER *and*
PRINCESS LEIA *on balcony.*

LEIA   I prithee, say: what is the matter, Luke?

LUKE   Between who?

LEIA   —Nay, the matter on your heart.

LUKE   Say, dost thou of thy mother yet retain   275
         A memory? I fain would hear thee tell.

LEIA   But little, Luke, for I was all too young
         When she departed to her resting place.

LUKE   Yet what dost thou remember? Wilt thou share?

LEIA   'Tis mostly images I see within   280
         My mind when I do think on her, just as
         The reds and oranges that one doth see
         When one hath look'd upon the shining sun.
         She was a woman of great beauty who
         Was kind, yet nurs'd some sadness deep within.   285
         Now tell me, wherefore dost thou ask me this?

LUKE   No mem'ry have I of a mother's touch,
         Nor kindness, sadness, smile, or any speech.
         'Twas not until but recently I thought
         Upon my state of being motherless.   290

LEIA   What troubles thee, dear Luke?

LUKE   —Darth Vader's here,
         E'en now, upon this very forest moon.

LEIA   How dost thou know?

LUKE   —I felt his presence here.
         He cometh seeking me, for he can feel
         When I am near. This is why I must leave: 295
         As long as I remain I do the group
         And our good mission put at risk. Instead,

	My destiny it is to face the man.	
LEIA	But wherefore?	
LUKE	—He, e'en Vader, is my father.	
LEIA	Thy father? What base trick of Fate is this?	300
LUKE	This news is but the prologue to the rest	
	That I shall tell thee, Leia. This shall not	
	Fall easily upon thine ears, but thou	
	Must hear't: if I do not return, then thou	
	Shalt be the only hope for the Alliance.	305
LEIA	Nay, say not so, dear Luke! Thou hast a pow'r	
	I do not comprehend, and never could	
	Obtain. 'Tis far beyond my skill and means.	
LUKE	But there thou art mistaken, Leia: thou	
	Dost have that pow'r within thee, and, in time,	310
	Shall learn to use it as I have. The Force	
	Is strong and certain in my family.	
	My father has it, I have it as well,	
	And also doth my sister have it. Aye,	
	'Tis thee, dear Leia, sister of my soul.	315
LEIA	[aside:] A brother! What strange circumstance is this?	
	My friend, this Luke, doth claim a brother's place?	
	And is Darth Vader thus my father, too?	
	What of the father that I once did know—	
	Organa, he for whom I have been nam'd?	320
	Shall I, now fully grown, begin anew	
	And learn to love another family?	
	I thought my kinfolk all had been dispatch'd	
	When Alderaan was cruelly destroy'd.	
	Yet Luke doth tell me that the man who stood	325
	And watch'd with joy whilst Alderaan was blown	
	Apart is he whom I should "Father" call?	

       It shall take time and thought to reconcile
       My heart unto this news. But with what joy
       Already I do welcome Luke into   330
       My life as brother—there I have no qualms,
       For he hath been a brother unto me
       Since first we met. A brother! O, what news!
       [*To Luke:*] It is as if I did already know—
       Within my heart 'tis like I've always known.   335

LUKE   Then canst thou see why I must face him now?

LEIA   Nay, that I cannot see. If he can feel
       Thee here, then flee anon and save thy life!
       It is no shame to fly from danger, Luke.
       I wish that I could fly with thee.

LUKE   —Nay, say   340
       That not, for thou e'er wert the strongest one.

LEIA   But wherefore needest thou confront him, Luke?

LUKE   Methinks the man hath good within him still,
       And shall not basely render his own son
       Unto his cruel and vicious Emperor.   345
       Methinks I still can save the man who gave
       Us life, and turn him to the good once more.
       Methinks I must endeavor so to do,
       Or else my path is darker e'en than his.
       Methinks so many things, dear Leia, but   350
       The most important of them all is this:
       My father is my duty to reclaim,
       E'en though he has a vile existence led.
       His heart, his soul, his life can be redeem'd,
       'Tis now my mission and, I hope, thine too.   355
       And now farewell, for I must take my leave.

                        [Exit Luke Skywalker.

LEIA   O, what a noble mind is here reveal'd:
          My brother young, yet speaking like a man
          Imbu'd with ev'ry honorable trait.
          To take upon himself the role of nurse   360
          To heal our wayward, troubl'd father. Ah!
          And I, of ladies most profoundly bless'd,
          To have a brother such as this good Luke—
          His swift return unto our loyal band
          I shall with pride await. O joy is mine,   365
          T'have seen what I have seen, see what I see!

                    Enter HAN SOLO.

HAN   What ails thee, Leia?
LEIA   —Nothing, Han. I've grown
          More full of deepest feeling than I e'er
          Thought possible. I would remain alone
          Till I have time to ponder this affair.   370
HAN   'Tis "nothing"? Prithee, tell me what is wrong.
LEIA   Thou dost not see—I cannot tell thee yet.
HAN   But Luke, couldst thou tell Luke in whisper'd song?
          Then shall I leave thee.
LEIA   —O!
                              [Han Solo begins to leave, but then
                                    returns to Princess Leia.
HAN   —Beg pardon, pet.   375
          Forgive this latest outburst of my pride,
          I am but worried for thy state of mind.
LEIA   Embrace me, Han, and here with me abide:
          Thou art a man of substance, strong and kind.
                                    [They embrace.

HAN   Although thou causest me to fret and groan,   380
               My love is thine and thou shalt ne'er be lone.

                                                    [Exeunt.

SCENE 4.

The forest moon of Endor.

Enter DARTH VADER.

VADER   E'en now my son doth come to me, I feel't.
               Thus is the moment near when I bring him
               Unto my Lord and, in so doing, bind
               Together those two forces of my life:
               My skillful son and my true Emperor.   5
               The two become one: 'Tis a consummation
               Devoutly to be wish'd. I'll see Luke turn'd
               Toward the dark side of the Force, and we
               Shall rule the galaxy—the father, son,
               And mighty Emperor. O make it so,   10
               Most slippery and cunning Fate, for great
               Shall be the combination of our pow'rs.

               Enter LUKE SKYWALKER *and* IMPERIAL COMMANDER,
                       with STORMTROOPERS.

COMMAND.   My Lord, this is the rebel who did bring
               Himself to us in full surrender. He
               Denieth there are others here, yet I   15
               Believe there may be more. I do request
               Permission to conduct a search of the

Surrounding area. "No stone unturn'd,"
As my dear father us'd to say. Is not
A father's wisdom precious more than gold?   20
But I digress: the rebel came here arm'd
With this and this alone, a lightsaber.

                     [The Imperial commander hands
                     Luke's lightsaber to Darth Vader.

VADER   [*aside:*] O how it stirs my soul to hear him tell
        The love of his good father. Now, be calm!
        [*To commander:*] Thou hast fulfill'd thine office
                                 faithfully,   25
        Commander. Leave us now, conduct thy search,
        And bring this one's companions back to me.
        I'll warrant thou shalt find them as thou think'st.

COMMAND. Of course, my Lord. My pleasure 'tis to see
        Thy great will done. If further rebels are   30
        Upon the moon, we shall discover them.

                       [Exit Imperial commander.

VADER   The Emperor hath been expecting thee.
LUKE   [*aside:*] Now it begins. [*To Darth Vader:*] I know,
                             my father.

VADER   —Ah,
        Thou hast accepted what is true.
LUKE   —I have
        Accepted thou wert once call'd Anakin   35
        Skywalker, and as such, my father wert,
        And art, and whate'er come to pass, shall be.
VADER   That "Anakin" is meaningless to me.
        The name hath neither relevance nor worth.
        My life is chang'd, and I with it, fore'er.   40
LUKE   'Tis but the name of thy true self, which thou

Hast but forgotten. Furthermore, I know
That there is good within thee yet, for thy
Great Emperor cannot have driven it
From thee entirely. That is wherefore thou 45
Couldst not destroy me when we met at first,
And wherefore thou wilt not deliver me
A pris'ner to thine Emperor.

VADER [*aside:*] —Almost
I know not what to say, so shall I turn
The conversation unto matters that 50
Are simple to discuss, with no confusion.
[*To Luke:*] I see thou hast constructed for thyself
A lightsaber. Thy skills are now complete,
Except I see its beam is green, much like
Thine innocent opinion of my fate. 55
But still thou hast become quite powerful,
Just as the Emperor himself foresaw.

LUKE If green doth mark me as a man naïve,
I'll claim the color proudly. Come with me—
My father, turn toward the good, and live! 60

VADER Old Obi-Wan once thought as thou dost think.
Thou canst not understand the power of
The dark side: I shall be obedient
Unto my master—aye, I must, and will.

LUKE I shall not turn toward the dark, and thou 65
Shalt verily be forc'd to kill me then.

VADER [*aside:*] Confusion, be thou gone. 'Tis madness, this!
[*To Luke:*] If that shall be thy destiny, so be't.

LUKE O, search thy feelings, father. Thou canst not
Do this to me. I feel the conflict rise 70
Within thee. Let thy hatred go, be free!

VADER   It is too late for me, my son. I shall
          Deliver thee unto the Emperor.
          'Tis he who shall reveal to thee the true
          And pow'rful nature of the Force. He is   75
          Thy master now, and thou shalt serve him well.

LUKE   Then may I say these words with confidence:
          My father who once liv'd is truly dead.

                              [Exeunt Luke Skywalker with
                                   stormtroopers guarding.

VADER   O what a rogue and peasant Sith am I.
          This turmoil in my spirit doth not suit   80
          A dark and vicious warlord like myself.
          My son a rebel—fickle-minded Fate
          That e'er would be so cruel to have me see't!
          And not a simple rebel, nay, but he
          A hero, noble, brave, and true, a lad   85
          Whose character befits his parentage.
          Were he within the Empire's ranks employ'd,
          I would be proud to govern by his side.
          A worthy lad is he, of virtues full,
          A Jedi Knight and pow'rful in the Force,   90
          A brave, courageous, cunning warrior,
          A shadow of my former, noble self.
          Yet if he will not turn he'll be destroy'd.
          O shall it be? The strands of Fate do seem
          To wind themselves about my neck as if   95
          To strangle me and drag me down into
          The measureless, uncharted depths of my
          Beloved Emperor's most perfect will.
          Thus shall I drown within the dark side's pull:
          A murky grave to bury Vader's soul.   100

The rudder of my conscience runs not straight,
Thus am I tow'd along toward my Fate.

                                                [Exit.

SCENE 1.

The forest moon of Endor.

Enter HAN SOLO, PRINCESS LEIA, CHEWBACCA,
C-3PO, R2-D2, WICKET, PAPLOO,
and several REBELS.

LEIA   The entrance to the bunker where the Death
     Star's shield controllèd is lies just beyond
     That landing platform there. To get inside,
     Without revealing our intent shall not
     Be easy.

HAN   —Fear thou not. Chewbacca and   5
     Myself have enter'd places that were far
     More heavily protected than this one.
     The tales I could relate—another time.

WICKET   Na nubba nubba,
     Weeva nubba,   10
     Nozza wayza,
     Yubba yubba.

C-3PO   N'ketcha ketcha,
     Yuzza betcha,
     Yuzza surra,   15
     Netcha, netcha.

WICKET   Suki, suki,
     Nahgoh luki,
     Nahyoo siya,
     Ch'buki uki.   20

LEIA   I prithee, 3PO, what doth he say?

C-3PO   'Tis news that shall delight, good Princess, for

It renders our assault yet easier.
A secret entrance may be found along
The other side of this great ridge.

HAN   —'Tis well.   25
So let us hence and find this hidden way.
                 [*The group of rebels and Ewoks*
                        walks to a new location.

LEIA   [*aside:*] What circumstance unlikely doth befall—
A group of hardy rebels makes its way
Unto a battle with the Empire vile.
Such enterprise of pith and moment, yet   30
Here are we by these furry creatures led.
What unexpected allies! Aye, what strange
But needed friends these noble scamps may prove.
There is a saying back on Alderaan—
Or rather, should I say, there us'd to be   35
For now no sayings there are heard at all—
"There should for no one greater welcome be
Than one who is an unexpected guest."
So do we welcome these small ones unto
Our great and just Rebellion, these who are   40
Both meek and full of childlike eagerness.
Yet even as these words escape my lips,
Another thought unfolds itself to me:
It is not we who welcome them; I err.
For 'tis their moon, their home, their dwelling place.   45
'Tis surely they who kindly welcome us,
'Tis truly they to whom our thanks are due,
'Tis certain they are far more brave than we,
'Tis verily their home for which they fight.
But still thy tongue, the bunker now is near.   50

HAN   [*to Paploo:*] Thou hast a back door found, thy
                                          hairiness?
        'Tis well: from furry mouths come good ideas.

PAPLOO   [*to Wicket:*] Ba'chua ba'chua,
        Megoh ga'chua,
        Megoh gennem,   55
        Fa'chua, fa'chua.

Enter several IMPERIAL SCOUTS *near the bunker.*
Paploo walks toward them.

HAN   [*to Leia:*] There are not many guards nearby; to gain
        The upper hand should not prove difficult.

LEIA   And yet it needeth merely one to sound
        A loud alarm that brings the fleet entire.   60

HAN   Forsooth, then quietlike our moves shall be.

WICKET   [*to C-3PO:*] N'unka unka,
        Paploo flunka,
        Heeza gennem,
        Bunka, bunka.   65

C-3PO   O my! Good Princess Leia, I do fear
        Our small befurr'd companion hath set on
        An errand rash.

CHEWBAC.   —Auugh!
        [All watch as Paploo approaches the scouts.

LEIA   —Fie! The little beast
        Doth make his way unto a certain death.
        Belike these guards shall blast him into bits.   70

HAN   And further: our surprise attack is gone.
        We may not have another chance as this.
                      [Paploo suddenly boards a speeder

	bike and flies off into the distance.
SCOUT 1	Alack! That beast hath ta'en the speeder bike!
	We shall not let the imp steal from us so!
SCOUT 2	Let us fly hence and after him!
SCOUT 3	—Away! 75

         [Imperial Scouts 1, 2, and 3 mount
              their bikes and chase Paploo.

HAN   A clever ruse for one who is no more
           Than a mere lump of matted fur. He hath
           Succeeded in his plan, for now behold:
           Just one is left. [*To C-3PO:*] Remain here and await
           Our swift return.

C-3PO   —Though I am but a droid,   80
           My will is yet my own. I shall decide
           What course to take, and have decided it
           Shall better be if R2 and myself
           Remain here.

HAN   —Well consider'd, goldenrod.
           Now let us go, my friends, and make our way   85
           Unto the bunker. Guard, what ho?

         [Han Solo approaches another Imperial scout.

SCOUT 4   —Thou knave,
           What treachery is this?

         [Imperial Scout 4 runs after Han Solo
             but soon is surrounded by rebels.

HAN   —Such treachery
           As shall an Empire conquer. Now, avaunt,
           Thou scurvy servant of the Empire's spite!

         [The rebels subdue Imperial Scout 4.

LEIA   Good friends and rebels all, are you prepar'd?   90
           The moment is upon us, even now:

We shall the bunker enter sans delay,
And what we'll find therein we do not know.
Belike some danger grave doth wait inside,
Mayhap far worse than ever we imagine.   95
Be ready—eyes alert and open wide!
> [Han Solo, Chewbacca, Princess Leia, and rebels
> enter the bunker. Several Imperial troops are
> inside, surprised by the rebels' entrance.

HAN   Pray, mark me well, else all of you shall die:
Move quickly to the side, and let us in.
> [Imperial troops move away, surrounded by rebels.
Go, brave Chewbacca, guard these wayward souls.

LEIA   Make haste, good Han. The fleet shall be in range   100
Anon.

CHEWBAC.   —Egh, auugh!

HAN   —Give me those charges, quick!

> Enter more IMPERIAL TROOPS, COMMANDERS,
> and STORMTROOPERS, running into the bunker.
> C-3PO, still outside the bunker, sees them.

C-3PO   O my, they shall be captur'd! Misery!
If only I could quickly warn them all.

WICKET   Netah muah,
Meego thuah,   105
Meego gennem,
Puah, puah.
> [Exit Wicket in haste.

R2-D2   Beep, meep!

C-3PO   —Where dost thou go? Come back! R2,
Stay here with me, I pray. My joints and wires

Are burning with my terror and my fear.   110
If thou dost leave, I surely shall melt down
From all the dread that runs through me.
R2-D2   —Meep, squeak!
[*Aside*:] Though small, his brave protection shall I be!
We cannot save the others, and may not
E'en save ourselves, but I shall not, at least,   115
Desert C-3PO when he's afear'd.
COMMAND. [*to Han*:] Be still, thou rebel scum.
HAN   [*aside*:]   —Alas, how's this?
The Empire knew our plan—something's amiss!
[*Exeunt all, with Imperial troops subduing rebels.*

SCENE 2.
Inside the second Death Star.

Enter two GUARDS.

GUARD 1   Oi! Comrade, how art thou?
GUARD 2   —Quite well, my friend.
Say, didst thou hear the news?
GUARD 1   —What news, pray tell?
GUARD 2   It seemeth we have found Skywalker.
GUARD 1   —Aye?
The lad for whom we have for ages search'd?
The one o'er whom Darth Vader seems obsess'd?   5
The mighty boy of whom we've all been warn'd?
GUARD 2   Indeed, the same—thou knowest whom I mean.
GUARD 1   Where was he, then?
GUARD 2   —Upon the moon.

GUARD 1   —Which moon?

GUARD 2   The moon around which we do orbit now.
            E'en Endor.

GUARD 1   —Can it be? Our enemy,   10
            The greatest threat the Empire's ever known,
            Hath 'scaped our watch and is to Endor flown?
            How can that be, for do we not have guards
            Identifying ev'ry ship that comes?
            Hath he fool'd them to make his landing, then?   15

GUARD 2   E'en so. Lord Vader hath return'd with him.

GUARD 1   Darth Vader brought him here?

GUARD 2   —Yes. Wherefore art
            Thou so perplex'd?

GUARD 1   —The rebel pilot who
            Hath single-handedly destroy'd the first
            Death Star is hither brought—

GUARD 2   —As prisoner.   20

GUARD 1   As prisoner. Aye, that is better. But
            How came he then to be on Endor, say?
            And wherefore was he there? Do we yet know?

GUARD 2   How he hath landed there is yet beyond
            Our knowing. He hath said he was alone.   25

GUARD 1   And hath he been believ'd?

GUARD 2   —Nay, we have not
            Our senses quite forgot. Pray, give our men
            An ounce of credit, lad. Our scouts do search
            For his accomplices e'en now.

GUARD 1   —'Tis well.

GUARD 2   Forsooth, the Empire soon shall triumph.

GUARD 1   —But . . .   30

GUARD 2   Alas, my friend, what troubles thee? Why dost

	Thou speak this "but"? Why "but"? What "but"?	
GUARD 1	—Hast thou	
	Read the descriptions of the Endor moon?	
GUARD 2	I have, for we were order'd so to do.	
GUARD 1	Then thou hast heard about the creatures there.	35
GUARD 2	Mean'st thou the native population that	
	Was deemèd insignificant?	
GUARD 1	—Indeed.	
	The full report hath said that they are arm'd.	
GUARD 2	But with such sticks and rocks as would not harm	
	A womp rat, and much less an AT-AT. Thou	40
	Wilt not fear armies made of twigs. 'Tis true?	
GUARD 1	Perhaps, yet follow on: it seems that there	
	Are rebels on the forest moon, who now	
	Have hidden, and we know not where. What if	
	These rebels were to meet the creatures, band	45
	Together, crush the bunker that controls	
	The shield that watcheth o'er the Death Star, then	
	Coordinate a wing'd assault, which would	
	Destroy this battle station and—still more—	
	Deliver our dread Emperor and Lord	50
	Darth Vader unto their untimely deaths?	
	Could not just such a chain of dire events	
	Defeat the Empire strong in one fell swoop?	
GUARD 2	Thou shouldst not be a guard, my friend, for thou	
	Art suited for a life of fantasy.	55
	Thou shouldst a writer be of stories grand	
	Wherein a group of men and simple beasts	
	Do overthrow an Empire powerful.	
	O, it doth break upon my sight: my friend,	
	The ancient storyteller he, who weaves	60

His tales to bring delight to all who hear.

GUARD 1   Thou mockest me.

GUARD 2   —Well notic'd! Mark me now:
Thy fears all rest upon a tiny word,
A word so small it should not give thee cause
To fret and worry so: that word is "if."   65
"If" there were rebels on the forest moon,
"If" they did meet with creatures and form pacts,
"If" then they could our bunker strong destroy,
"If" they had plann'd to strike our Death Star great.
Thine "if" itself the Empire overthrows,   70
But "if" knows little of reality.
I tell thee true, if I had richer been,
If I had been a politician's son,
If I were rais'd in wealth and privilege,
If I myself became most powerful,   75
Why then, I would be Emperor, not guard!
But for the "ifs."

GUARD 1   —Thy point is made, and I
Shall rest my "ifs" and be at ease. Now, if
Thou shalt come with me, we have both been call'd
To rearrange the chairs upon the deck.   80

GUARD 2   If thou shalt lead, I'll follow, worthy friend.

                                            [Exeunt.

                    Enter EMPEROR PALPATINE
                 on balcony, with ROYAL GUARDS.

EMPEROR   Our age is but a constant grasp for pow'r,
A time when trust and honor are no more
And all is but a furious race till death.

How doth a person make a life that's worth   85
The living? Is't by love or ventures? Nay:
The one who hath the greatest pow'r prevails.
The politicians grumble, scrape, and grab,
A'fighting o'er their spheres of influence,
The people cringe and whimper 'neath the loads   90
Plac'd on them by those in authority,
And all in bleak timidity do cow'r
When in the presence of their Emperor.
O what a piece of work are we! I should
Find joy in our humanity, and yet,   95
To me, what is this quintessence of dust?
A galaxy of vermin searching for
A crumb of what the best do eat, all rul'd
By those who have the appetite for pow'r—
For in a world of darkness only those   100
Who serve the dark deserve to live and thrive.
Let those naïve and wayward souls who seek
For justice, wisdom, honesty, and right
Endure such suffering as fits their weak
And simple souls. Let those who love be made   105
To witness how their lov'd ones scream and shriek
And, at the last, forsake e'en those they love
When tortur'd by the mighty hand of pow'r.
Let those who lurch and stumble t'ward the light
Discover, in the moments ere they die,   110
The light they sought is but a blaster shot,
Lightsaber beam or lightning of the Sith
That shall their wretched life put to an end.
And let the vile Rebellion choke upon
Its own absurd and innocent ideals,   115

Until each sick'ning, cursèd, backward soul
Who e'er hath spoken in Rebellion's name
Lies broken in the streets, beneath my steps.
Aye, let's kill all the rebels. It shall be,
For power is my slave and I its god.   120

         Enter LUKE SKYWALKER *and*
         DARTH VADER *on balcony.*

I bid thee welcome, young Skywalker. Long
Have I awaited thee. Guards, leave us now.
                [Exeunt royal guards.
I do look forward to the moment when
Thy training shall completed be. In time
Thou shalt bow low and call me Master.
LUKE   —There   125
Thou art mistaken gravely, for I am
Not thine to be converted as thou in
The past did turn my father.
EMPEROR   —Nay, my young
Apprentice. Thou shalt find 'tis thou who art
Mistaken vis-à-vis so many things.   130
    [Darth Vader hands Luke's lightsaber to the Emperor.
VADER   His lightsaber I give to thee.
EMPEROR   —Indeed.
The weapon of a Jedi Knight, much like
Thy father. Surely, boy, thou knowest well
That never shall thy father turnèd be
Away from dark toward the good; so shall   135
It be for thee.
LUKE   —O, thou art wrong. Anon

I shall be dead, and thou with me.
EMPEROR   —Ha, ha!
          Belike thou speakest of the imminent
          Attack that hath been plannèd by the fleet
          Of rebel ships?
LUKE   [*aside:*] —Alas! How can he know?   140
EMPEROR   Aye, let me reassure thee we are safe
          Here from the foolish undertaking of
          Thy wretched friends.
LUKE   —Thine overconfidence
          Is thy great weakness.
EMPEROR   —And thy faith in thy
          Base friends is thine.
VADER   —'Tis pointless to resist,   145
          My son. Thou shalt be turn'd unto the dark,
          And then we three shall rule the galaxy.
EMPEROR   Dost thou not see? All that hath happen'd doth
          Proceed according to my grand design.
          Thy friends upon the sanctuary moon   150
          Now walk into a trap that I shall spring.
          Thy rebel fleet as well: the snare is set
          To catch the pests and crush them 'twixt my fingers.
          Hast thou yet understood? 'Twas I who did
          Allow thy bold Alliance to find out   155
          The site of the shield generator; it
          Is wholly safe from thy band pitiful.
          I let thy spies believe they had reveal'd
          A secret great about this station, yet
          'Twas I who leak'd intelligence to them,   160
          So all the pieces would be perfectly
          Arrang'd to strike rebellion down at last.

A legion of my finest troops awaits
Their piteous attack. But O, fear not,
For fully operational the shield   165
Shall be when thy misguided friends arrive.
With skill the players all are put in place,
Much bloodshed and destruction shall they face.

                         [Exeunt.

SCENE 3.

Space / Inside the second Death Star.

Enter CHORUS.

CHORUS   Imagine you see space, ye viewers true,
In which the final battle shall be fought.
The rebels put their trust i'the Endor crew:
Unless the shield is down, 'tis all for naught.
Yet little do they know that plan hath fail'd,   5
For Palpatine hath work'd his great deceit.
On Endor is the rebel crew assail'd,
Which doth create disaster for the fleet.

                         [Exit chorus.

Enter LANDO OF CALRISSIAN, NIEN NUNB,
ADMIRAL ACKBAR, WEDGE ANTILLES,
and other REBEL PILOTS.

LANDO   Great Admiral, we're in position now.
Each rebel fighter is accounted for,   10
And all are now prepar'd for our attack.

ACKBAR   Proceed, then, with the countdown in a snap.

NIEN   [*to Lando:*] Ungate-oh ah theyairee uhareh
           Mu-ah-hareh. Mu-ah-hareh mu-kay?

LANDO   Nay, worry not, my strangely membran'd friend.   15
           My friend, the valiant Han, shall play his part,
           And shall the shield disable in good time.

NIEN   Emutee bitchu me.

LANDO   [*aside:*]   —Or this shall be
           The shortest onslaught we will e'er attempt.

ACKBAR   All groups assume attack coordinates,   20
           And craft prepare to jump to hyperspace
           When I have giv'n the sign to make it hap'.
                      [The ships jump to hyperspace.

LANDO   Now we approach the Death Star, Admiral.
           The moment hath arriv'd for us to strike
           And win the day in grand Rebellion's name.   25
           All wings, I prithee, make report.

WEDGE   —'Tis I,
           Red Leader, standing by.

GRAY LEAD.   —Gray Leader doth
           Stand by.

GREEN LEAD.   —'Tis I, Green Leader standing by.

WEDGE   Now lock thine S-foils in attacking mode.

ACKBAR   And may the Force be with us in this scrap.   30

WEDGE   [*aside:*] Like thee, dear friends, I have observer been
           Of all this great Rebellion for a time.
           Yet I have also been participant,
           And fortunate enough to keep my life
           E'en when full many others have expir'd.   35
           The first grave Death Star battle I did see,
           All ships but Luke's and mine were cruelly wreck'd.

I dwelt within the rebels' base on Hoth,
Where I fac'd AT-ATs in the snowy fight.
The second Death Star shall I here confront,   40
But know not whether I shall live or die.
Still, my life is but little consequence,
For though it ever in grave danger be,
I know I play a mere supporting part
Unto the greater cause of this Rebellion.   45
I am an actor in a drama vast—
A witness to the tragedy and hope,
The pain, the joy, the sadness, and the fear
That ever follow bold Rebellion's name.
Like thee, I wonder how the tale will end,   50
And who shall live to see the glorious day
When falls the curtain on the Empire's might.
Until that day I shall be on the scene,
To play my part as pilot: faithful, true,
Committed to the play that doth play out,   55
Determin'd to help write our final act—
To lift our noble cause e'en by a Wedge.

NIEN   [to Lando:] Lamou-be-o-tee?
LANDO   —But what dost thou mean?
We must be able to detect the shield,
Whether 'tis up or down.

NIEN   —Na mateeou.   60

LANDO   How could the Empire jam our scan, unless
They knew that we were coming—O, alas!
What awful understanding hath just now
Broke in upon mine unsuspecting mind!
I see now we are caught—break off th'attack!   65
The shield is up.

WEDGE   —I get no reading, Sir.
              Canst thou be sure?
LANDO   —Pull up, good men, pull up!
                                  [The rebels begin to change course
                                  and retreat from the Death Star.
ACKBAR   Prepare to take evasive action! Heed
              My words, ye pilots all. Green Team, hear now:
              Stay close to sector MV-7 on   70
              The map.
CONTROL.   —Good admiral, approaching ships!
              It is the enemy.
ACKBAR   —O knavery
              Most vile, O trick of Empire's basest wit.
              A snare, a ruse, a ploy: and we the fools.

What great deception hath been plied today—   75
O rebels, do you hear? Fie, 'tis a trap!

Enter IMPERIAL PILOTS.
They begin to duel with the rebels.

LANDO   The fighters come upon us!
PILOT 1   —Woe is me,
           There are too many! O, what shall we do?
LANDO   Accelerate to full attacking speed.
           Be sure thou draw their fire far from the cruisers.   80
WEDGE   I copy and obey, Gold Leader.

Enter LUKE SKYWALKER, DARTH VADER, *and* EMPEROR PALPATINE
*above on balcony watching the battle as rebels and
Imperial pilots exeunt.*

EMPEROR   —Come,
           My boy, and see what doth befall thy friends.
           From here thou shalt bear witness to the end—
           The final, whole destruction of the weak
           Alliance, and Rebellion's ruin, too.   85
           How stir thy feelings now, apprentice mine?
LUKE   [*aside:*] What torment fills my soul! Shall I take up
           My lightsaber and so destroy this man?
           Be still, else by my thoughts I am betray'd.
EMPEROR   This lightsaber that resteth by my side—   90
           Thou dost desire it hotly, dost thou not?
           The hate doth swell within thee even now—
           It hath an aura palpable. Take up
           Thy Jedi weapon, use it. I—as thou

Canst see—am quite unarm'd. So strike me down   95
With all thy hatred, let thine anger stir.
Each moment thou dost more become my slave.

LUKE   Nay, thou shalt not condemn me to the dark.
My father's tragic fate shall not be mine.

EMPEROR   'Tis unavoidable. 'Tis destiny.   100
No person ever dodg'd their final fate,
Or kept the sands of time from flowing free.
Thou shalt not 'scape the bounds of providence,
Or trick the whims of fortune's fickle wheel.
So hear these words and well believe them, boy: 105
Thou now art mine, just as thy father is.
Together we are powerful, we three—
When thou art turn'd, we'll rule the galaxy.

                                        [Exeunt.

ACT V

SCENE 1.

The forest moon of Endor.

Enter HAN SOLO, PRINCESS LEIA, CHEWBACCA, *and several*
REBELS *guarded by* IMPERIAL TROOPS, COMMANDERS,
CONTROLLERS, *and multiple* AT-ST IMPERIAL WALKERS.

TROOPER 1 [*to Han:*] Thou rebel dog, move quickly, lest thou die.
　　　　　　Forsooth, 'twould give me pleasure to destroy
　　　　　　Thee, and would bring a great reward, as well.

HAN　　　　[*to Leia:*] This mission, it would seem, hath fail'd,
　　　　　　　　　　　　　　　　　　　　　　　　　　　'less there
　　　　　　Is yet some unknown force to rescue us.　　　　　5

LEIA　　　　We must have confidence—all is not lost.
　　　　　　E'en in the darkest hour we may have hope—
　　　　　　Experience hath taught me thus, for once
　　　　　　I did lose thee, which was far worse than this.

Enter C-3PO *and* R2-D2.

C-3PO　　　What, ho! I say, ye stormtroopers, were you　　　10
　　　　　　A'searching for me and my mate?

HAN　　　　　　　—The droid,
　　　　　　What is his game? I hope the silly fool
　　　　　　Knows what he does.

CHEWBAC.　　　　　　　　—Auugh!

COMMAND.　　　　　　　　　　　—Bring those two to me!
　　　　　　I'll not be mock'd by droids whilst I have breath.
　　　　　　　　　　　[*The stormtroopers rush toward the droids.*

| C-3PO | They speed to us anon. I say, R2, | 15 |

C-3PO   They speed to us anon. I say, R2,   15
           Art thou assur'd this is a good idea?
R2-D2   Beep, whistle, meep! [*Aside:*] Thou soon shalt see,
                                        my friend,
           How well I have consider'd this idea.
           For though the furry creatures harmless seem,
           And though I am a simple, squeaking droid,   20
           Together we've a cunning strategy.
TROOPER 2   Now freeze, ye wayward droids! And do not move!
C-3PO   Most heartily I grant thee my surrender.

> [*The stormtroopers reach the droids. As they begin*
> *to take the droids to the other rebels, Ewoks enter*
> *from every corner of the stage to fight the*
> *Imperial troops. The Ewoks blow horned*
> *instruments to signal the attack.*

HAN   What sound is this? The call of horns and fife!
           The battle hath begun in earnest with   25
           A fairer balance of the rival sides.
           Those noble little creatures have arriv'd
           To bear the standard of our worthy cause.
           What loud commotion hath their coming made—
           Now arrows fly from their well-aimèd bows,   30
           And hit the mark—the troops fall left and right.
           O sit thee back no more, Han, take thy stand!
           Let courage stir within my smuggler's blood!

> [*Han begins fighting the Imperial*
> *troops around him.*

LEIA   O bravely met, good friends, fight on! Now Han,
           We must unto the bunker and renew   35
           Our effort to make entrance and destroy
           The shield that still about the Death Star lies.

                    We represent Rebellion's greatest hope!
                        [*Han and Leia make their way to the bunker. Exit*
                            Chewbacca, fighting. R2-D2 watches the battle
                                from the other side of the stage.

R2-D2   [*aside:*] See how the creatures fight! What skill and wit
                    They use to struggle 'gainst their foes. There is   40
                    One flying through the sky on wings of bark,
                    Who drops upon the walker his small load.
                    The AT-ST doth not feel the hit,
                    But O, what daring hath the creature shown!
                    A group doth hold a rope across the path   45
                    To trip a walker up, yet it but pulls
                    Them all along. Yet some have triumph'd, too,
                    For they have crush'd a walker's cockpit with
                    Two trunks of trees sent swinging from the vines.
                    Another gang employs large catapults   50
                    To send vast boulders hurtling through the sky.
                    Still others choose small stones to slay the troops,
                    And bash their helmets in with utmost glee.
                    There's one who takes a rock upon a string,
                    And tries to fling it t'ward a trooper's head,   55
                    But hath instead his own small visage hit.
                    What gallantry of spirit have these beasts.
                    E'en if their efforts sometimes are in vain,
                    They do what I, encas'd in steel, may not:
                    They put their bodies fully in the fight.   60

LEIA   [*to Han:*] The code unto the bunker door hath
                                                    chang'd!
                    We need R2!

HAN   —The terminal is here.
                    If he can make it o'er, this is his means

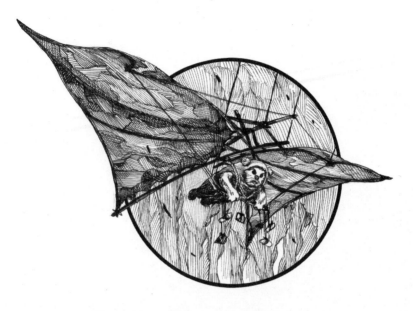

To swiftly open up the closèd door.

LEIA   R2, where art thou? Come to us anon!   65

R2-D2   [*to C-3PO:*] Beep, squeak!

C-3PO   —Thou goest? Wait, what dost thou mean?
I thought thou hadst resolvèd to remain.

R2-D2   Meep, whistle, hoo, beep, meep.

C-3PO   —But going where?
Pray patience, R2, this is not a time
For brave heroics! Hither now, return!   70

           [*The droids move toward Han Solo
                 and Princess Leia.*

R2-D2   Beep, squeak!

C-3PO   —We come, we come!

HAN   —I prithee, swift!

        [*R2-D2 plugs into the bunker door's control panel.*

LEIA   Quick, good R2—thou art our only hope.
                    [A stormtrooper shoots and hits R2-D2,
                    who is thrown backward, short-circuiting.
R2-D2   Hoo!
C-3PO   —R2, wherefore wert thou passing brave?
HAN   That plan, then, shall not be. Mayhap I can
            Still hot-wire these controls to ope the door.   75
LEIA   Good cover shall I give thee whilst thou work'st.

            Enter CHEWBACCA *and two* EWOKS, *aside, swinging*
                onto the top of an AT-ST Imperial walker.

CHEWBAC.   Auugh-egh-egh-auugh!
                    [Chewbacca and the Ewoks land on top of
                    the AT-ST. The AT-ST pilot and copilot see
                    an Ewok in the front screen.
AT-ST PILOT   —Pray, get the beastie off!
                [The AT-ST copilot opens the hatch and is thrown
                out by Chewbacca. The Ewoks enter the cockpit
                    and subdue the AT-ST pilot.
EWOK   N'mayta mayta,
            Heeza hayta,
            Weeza gonnem,   80
            Bayta, bayta.
                    [Chewbacca and the Ewoks begin piloting the
                        AT-ST toward the bunker, shooting Imperial
                    troops and destroying other AT-STs as they go.
HAN   The wiring have I reckon'd, and we shall
            Make entrance to the bunker presently.
            A-ha, 'tis done, and now the door's unlock'd!
                    [A second blast door shuts.

Have I been mock'd by cords and circuitry?   85
Shall I by wires and cable bested be?

          [A stormtrooper shoots Princess Leia in the
                    shoulder. Han Solo rushes to her side.

LEIA   Alack!

HAN   —My love, my heart, my very life!
I beg thee, tell me thou art well, and that
This wound shall not take what I hold most dear:
E'en thee. Shall this the final moment be,   90
Shall I live all my life in grave regret
That never did I tell thee what thou mean'st,
Or how completely thou hast won me o'er?
A smuggler's heart thou hast with cunning seiz'd,
A pirate's soul thou hast by kindness ta'en.   95
A scoundrel's life thou holdest hostage, chuck.
Thus, though I am by trade a smuggling man,
'Tis thou art guilty of a greater crime:
For thou dost practice larceny in love.

LEIA   I almost wish my wound were worse to hear   100
More of thy tender and most soothing words.
But truly, Han, I am not badly hurt.

          [The Imperial troops have all been defeated, except
                two stormtroopers approaching from behind.

TROOPER 2 Be still!

C-3PO   —O my!

TROOPER 2   —Move not, or else thou diest!

          [Princess Leia takes out her blaster discreetly,
                  preparing to shoot.

HAN   O, I do love thee, Leia dear.

LEIA   —I know.

          [Princess Leia shoots both stormtroopers.

HAN   Well aim'd, my sweet.

C-3PO   —Hurrah! We now are sav'd.   105

                      [The AT-ST piloted by Chewbacca
                           and the Ewoks approaches.

HAN   O, 'tis unjust! Another fighter yet?

               This battle fierce we very nearly won,

               Yet now this final vehicle appears.

               How shall we conquer it and still defeat

               The too-importunate Imperi'l threat?   110

               Shall we have no relief from enemies?

CHEWBAC.   *[emerging from the hatch:]* Auugh!

HAN   —Chewie! Blessèd sight art thou. I pray,

               Come quickly down, for she is wounded.

CHEWBAC.   —Egh!

HAN   Nay, wait! *[To Leia:]* A keen idea hath come to me,

               Which shall unto this doorway be our key.   115

                                 [Exeunt.

SCENE 2.

Space / Inside the second Death Star.

Enter LANDO OF CALRISSIAN, NIEN NUNB, ADMIRAL ACKBAR,
WEDGE ANTILLES, *and* OTHER REBEL PILOTS, *dueling with* IMPERIAL
TROOPS *in their ships. Enter* LUKE SKYWALKER, DARTH VADER, *and*
EMPEROR PALPATINE *on balcony, watching the battle below.*

LANDO   Take care, good Wedge: three come at thee above!

WEDGE   Red Three, Red Two, I prithee, pull ye in!

RED 2   I hear thy word and do attend, good Sir.

RED 3   Now three approach at twenty, by degrees.

WEDGE	Cut to the left; the leader is for me.	5
	Toward the frigate medical they fly—	
	O villainy, to make assault upon	
	Our injur'd. Nay, they shall not strike us thus!	
LANDO	I fly with thee, good Wedge, they'll not prevail.	
	But wait, what omen vile's before mine eyes?	10
	The fighters of the Empire are engag'd,	
	Yet all the Star Destroyers are at rest.	
	It is as though some show is here devis'd,	
	And we're the actors in a play of war.	

Enter ADMIRAL PIETT *and* IMPERIAL COMMANDER, *aside.*

COMMAND.	We're set in the position for attack.	15
PIETT	'Tis well, now hold thee fast, and wait.	
COMMAND.	—But Sir,	
	Dost mean that we shall not make our assault?	
PIETT	This is no plan of my invention, but	
	The edict cometh from the Emperor	
	Himself. He hath a special plan afoot.	20
	Our role here is but to prevent escape.	
	Hast thou mark'd well what I have said?	
COMMAND.	—Aye, Sir.	
	[*Exeunt Admiral Piett and Imperial commander.*	
EMPEROR	[*to Luke:*] As thou canst see, my young apprentice, all	
	Thy friends have fail'd. Now for the final blow:	
	Thou shalt bear witness to the strong firepow'r	25
	Of this both fully operational	
	And armèd battle station. [*Into comlink:*] Fire at will,	
	Commander! Let the rebels shriek with pain!	
	Excitement courses through my veins, for I	

Do thrill at bringing others misery.   30
       [*The Death Star shoots, sending beams across*
                   the stage and killing some rebel pilots.

LUKE   [*aside:*] O pierce my soul, thou cursèd hand of Fate!
Am I the cause for this most bitter scene?
The Death Star active while my comrades die,
And all that I may gaze upon their end.
How shall I keep my mind from thoughts most dark?   35
How shall I patient be when fac'd with this?
How shall I not respond to anger's call?
How shall I show a Jedi's noble soul?
Be with me, trusted Yoda and dear Ben,
Forsooth, I need you more than ever now.   40

LANDO   [*to Nien:*] That blast hath emanated from the Death

Star. O! 'Tis operational. [*Into comlink:*] Home One,
This is Gold Leader. Hast thou seen that blast?

ACKBAR   We did indeed, and our decision's made.
            All rebel fighters for retreat prepare—   45
            Our fleet is not sufficient to withstand
            The might of this new Death Star's thunderclap.

LANDO   Thou shalt not have another chance as this
            To mount attack upon the Empire, Sir.

ACKBAR   We've no choice, General Calrissian.   50
            Their vast firepow'r our ships cannot repel—
            Betwixt our strength and theirs, too wide's the gap!

LANDO   But still I trust that Han will soon disarm
            The shield. We must but give him time enough!
            His mission is no easier than ours.   55
            A thought hath come to me that we may use—
            'Tis dangerous, but may yet worthy prove.
            All ships move closer to the Star Destroy'rs,
            Engage the giant ships at point-blank range.

ACKBAR   At that close range, we'll not last long against   60
            A Star Destroyer's harsh and vicious rap.

LANDO   Yet shall we fare far better than we will
            If we engage the Death Star! And belike
            Our deaths shall mean their deaths as well. Lay on!
            [*Lando of Calrissian, Nien Nunb, Admiral Ackbar,*
            Wedge Antilles and all rebels and Imperial pilots
            begin to exit as they duel, while Luke Skywalker,
            Darth Vader, and Emperor Palpatine
            watch from above.

EMPEROR   Thy fleet hath lost, and thy dear ones upon   65
            The Endor moon shall not survive. Indeed,
            My troops shall make them squeal in agony.

There's nothing left for which to fight, and no
Escape for thee, my young apprentice. Thine
All'ance shall be destroy'd, as shall thy friends.   70
The cry of dying rebels—O, how sweet!
How like a song unto my spirit dark.
And now, young one, I feel thine anger rise.
I sense thy hatred, which doth stir my blood.
I sit here, all defenseless, in thy sight.   75
Take up thy weapon now, and strike me down
In all thy hate, and then your journey t'ward
The dark side of the Force shall be complete.

LUKE [*aside:*] This man is pure incarnate evil. Shall
He goad me past the point of no return?   80
But what else can I do? Shall I remain
And weakly watch the death of all I love?
Nay, I cannot—for I would rather die
Than live and know I did not fight for them.
I must have courage now, and come what may!   85

[*Luke reaches out toward his lightsaber with the
Force, drawing it into his hand. He tries to
strike the Emperor but is stopped by
Darth Vader's lightsaber.*

EMPEROR Ha, ha! Thy transformation hath begun!
Your steps draw ever closer unto me.

[*Luke Skywalker and Darth Vader duel.*

LUKE [*aside:*] Now shall I fight, if fight I must to save
My friends so dear.

VADER [*aside:*]   —He is far stronger and
More subtly skill'd than when we last did meet.   90

[*Luke Skywalker kicks Darth Vader off the
balcony. Darth Vader stands up below, ready.*

EMPEROR   'Tis well, apprentice—thine aggressiveness
            Shall serve thee well. Let all thy hatred flow
            Within thee.
                        [Luke Skywalker turns off his lightsaber.
VADER   —Obi-Wan hath taught thee well.
LUKE   I shall not fight thee, Father.
                            [Darth Vader climbs the balcony
                                and strikes at Luke Skywalker.

VADER   —Unwise art
            Thou so to lower thy defenses, boy!   95
                        [They continue to duel. Luke Skywalker
                                jumps away from Darth Vader.

            [Aside:] His nimbleness astounds me. Almost do
            I wish I did not serve another's will.
            Imagine what we two could do, were I
            Not subject to another's ev'ry whim.
LUKE   Thy thoughts betray thee, Father. I can feel   100
            The good within thee, and the conflict, too.
VADER   There is no conflict.
LUKE   —Aye, thou couldst not bring
            Thyself to kill me earlier and I
            Believe thou shalt not hurt me, even now.
VADER   Thou verily dost underestimate   105
            The power of the dark side. If thou wilt
            Not fight, then thou shalt meet thy destiny.
                        [Darth Vader throws his lightsaber toward
                                Luke Skywalker, which hits the balcony
                                where Luke stands. Luke falls and hides.

EMPEROR   Ha ha, 'tis well! Now, Vader: finish it.
VADER   *[aside:]* What words shall I employ to find a son,
            To drive him so to hatred that he shall   110

Attempt to strike me down, and then be turn'd
Unto the dark side? O, is this not strange?
Were e'er there words to such a purpose put?
[*To Luke:*] Thou canst not hide forever, Luke.

LUKE   —I shall
Not fight thee.

VADER   —Give thyself unto the dark   115
Side. 'Tis the only way to help thy friends.
[*Aside:*] O what is this I sense within him now?
Another secret kept conceal'd from me?
Shall I e'er be the last to know my past?
[*To Luke:*] Indeed, thy thoughts betray thee, for thou
                                                          hast   120
Strong feelings for thy friends, especially
For one thou dost call sister. Aye, thou hast
A sister, and a twin. Thy feelings have
Betray'd her too. 'Twas wise of Obi-Wan
To try to hide the girl from me, but now   125
His vast and utter failure is complete.

LUKE   [*aside:*] O Leia, how my thoughts have giv'n thee o'er!
Fie, cursèd be my weak and changing mind
That e'er I did let Vader see its thoughts.
I wish'd that he would but as father see   130
His daughter there, and by her presence might
Be mov'd toward a better, nobler path.
But now I know he doth but wish to taunt
And draw me out by his discovery.
O Leia, ever since I first did see   135
Thee in the beam from R2's light I knew
We shar'd a deep connection. Now have I
Been partner to her cause through many times

Of hardship: battles won and lost, the joys
That come from victory, and all the griefs   140
That flow when friends have perish'd. With regard
To this both noble and fair princess, I
Have gone from hope of romance to a far
More deep and greater form of love. I fain
Would give my life for her. But O! That I   145
Should here betray her so, e'en with my weak
And simple-minded thoughts—what folly! Nay,
Far more: what horrid, selfish knavery!
But how shall he, my father, use this knowledge?
Will he attempt to capture her again   150
And lock her in this Death Star as he hath
Before? Or shall he seek to kill her now,
Since he doth know she may a threat become?

VADER   Belike, boy, thou dost wonder how her fate
Shall alter'd be, since I do know of her.   155
Thus pay good heed to this I do declare:
If thou shalt not toward the dark side turn,
Mayhap she will.

LUKE   [*aside:*]   —O thought more evil than
Whate'er I did or could imagine. [*Revealing himself:*]
                                   Nay!
          [*Luke Skywalker fights Darth Vader passionately.*
For Leia shall I strike thee down, thou brute!   160
For Han and all my friends I do attack!
For Ben, whom thou didst slaughter sans remorse,
For all thou hast destroy'd, I vengeance bring!
               [*Luke Skywalker strikes Darth Vader
                         and cuts off his hand.*

VADER   Ah!

EMPEROR   —Good, my young apprentice. Thy strong hate
                   Hath made thee powerful, indeed. Fulfill   165
                   Thy destiny, and take thy father's place
                   Beside me. Strike him down, and rule with me!
                   [Luke Skywalker looks at the stump of Darth Vader's
                   *   hand, and at his own gloved hand.*

LUKE   [*aside:*] My father's hand, of wires and circuits made,
                   I have in fury sever'd quite. And here,
                   My hand, of wires and circuits also made,   170
                   For in another duel, another place,
                   He hath the living one dismember'd.
                   'Tis plain to me what is transpiring here:
                   I do become like him. Torn up by hate,
                   More like machine than man with ev'ry scar,   175
                   Fulfilling the foul Emperor's base will.
                   Shall this obsess'd, derang'd, and wicked man
                   Lead yet another Skywalker unto
                   A path of dark and evil? Shall it be
                   That I become the thing that I despise?   180
                   Protect me, Jedi ancestors, from such
                   A mangl'd Fate, so hopeless, grim and bleak.
                   [*To Emperor:*] I never shall be turn'd unto the dark.
                   Thy plan hath fail'd, thy Highness; I am Luke
                   Skywalker, Jedi Knight, just like my brave   185
                   And noble father.

EMPEROR   —Then so be it, Jedi.
                   Thy proclamations foolish change not this:
                   I still control thy final destiny.
                   If thou shalt not be turn'd, then thou shalt be
                   Destroy'd! Bear witness to the terror and   190
                   The torment of the dark side of the Force!

[*Emperor Palpatine strikes Luke Skywalker*
with lightning that flows through his hands.
Luke falls. Darth Vader rises.

LUKE   O agony!

EMPEROR   —Young fool, 'tis only now
In this, thy final living moment, thou
Dost comprehend thy folly and my might.
              [*He continues to strike Luke with lightning.*
Thy feeble skills are nothing when compar'd   195
To all the power of the dark side. Thou
Dost pay the rightful price for thy severe
And utter lack of vision. Aye, thy debt
Is due, and I am both thy creditor
And thy collector, too. What thou hast not   200
Repaid with thy belief I shall exact
From thine own flesh. And O, what joy it brings
To charge thee thus—my payment justly earn'd.
To wound thee, hurt thee, break thee, and, at last,
To bring to thee the death that I am ow'd.   205
              [*The Emperor continues to assault*
                    Luke with lightning.

LUKE   O, Father, please, do not stand idly by—
Assist me, if thou ever mercy knew!

EMPEROR   And now, young Luke Skywalker, thou shalt die.
              [*The Emperor gleefully assails Luke with*
                    lightning. Luke screams and writhes in pain.

LUKE   My Father, gracious father, lend me aid!
Extend to me the grace I beg of thee!   210

VADER   [*aside:*] This torment is not only his, but mine.
His ev'ry shriek doth sound within my soul
As though 'twere I who were assaulted here.

What feeling's this—my heart hath turn'd toward
The boy? My heart, that center of my soul   215
That I so long have hidden 'neath the dark
And evil deeds that well befit a Sith.
But how my heart doth groan as though it wakes
From lengthy sleep. It shakes my spirit, spurs
My aging wither'd body, and doth make   220
Me young again—I am a Jedi Knight,
By Obi-Wan instructed; Anakin,
The name by which my mother call'd me, calls
Me now to resurrect my former self.
Methinks I feel the Force within me here—   225
Not to perform the deeds of evil men
But to release myself from bitter hate
And rescue Luke, whose courage I behold.
It is the cause, it is the cause, my soul.
Be Anakin Skywalker now—recall   230
The man thou wert and rescue thy dear son!
            [Darth Vader lifts Emperor Palpatine and
                    throws him down a long shaft, where he is
                        killed amid his lightning and flames.

LUKE   O Father, thou hast sav'd me from great woe—
            And thou hast sav'd thyself. Now, let us go!
                                                    [Exeunt.

SCENE 3.

Inside the shield generator bunker on Endor /
Space / Inside the second Death Star.

Enter IMPERIAL COMMANDER *and* IMPERIAL TROOPS *on left side*

   of stage. Han Solo *appears in viewscreen, dressed as an*
         Imperial AT-ST pilot.

HAN   The battle's over, my commander. All
      The rebels have been routed, and abscond
      Unto the forest. Reinforcements are
      Requir'd to aid us in our quick pursuit.
TROOPS   Hurrah!
COMMAND. —Send thou three squads to bring them help! 5
      Pray, open up the back door speedily.
      What joy! The rebels know defeat today,
      And we'll rejoice to bear the news unto
      Our officers superior. Go now!
        [The Imperial troops open the back door and are
          met by Ewoks and rebels, who disarm them.
HAN   A cunning line! And you are quite the catch— 10
      Deceiv'd by rebels playing Empire's part!
      We dangled all your hopes for victory
      As bait to draw you in and hold you fast,
      And now we take the bunker in our care.
      Let fall your weapons, else I shall release 15
      Your lives unto these creatures' fearsome pow'r!
      Perchance they seem not vicious, yet they have
      What thou canst never know: fierce bravery.

  Enter Princess Leia *and* Chewbacca, *joined by* Han Solo,
  into the bunker. The Imperial troops remain guarded by the
        rebels at the back door.

LEIA   This bunker shall anon destroyèd be,
      And then our friends may strike their final blow. 20

HAN   Indeed! Pray, give to me another charge.
             We shall fulfill this task with perfect skill—
             And leave no charge unusèd.
CHEWBAC.   —Auugh!
LEIA   —'Tis set!
             Now let us fly! Else we shall bear the blast.
                         [Han Solo, Princess Leia, and Chewbacca
                         run from the bunker, which explodes.

             Enter LANDO OF CALRISSIAN, NIEN NUNB, ADMIRAL ACKBAR,
             WEDGE ANTILLES, *and other* REBEL PILOTS *on right side of stage,*
             dueling with IMPERIAL TROOPS *in their ships.* ADMIRAL PIETT
             and IMPERIAL CONTROLLER *are aside, inside the Death Star.*

ACKBAR   'Tis done, the Endor crew hath triumph'd yet—   25
             The shield is down! Upon the Death Star's main
             Reactor let us fly anon. Then shall
             We reach the core and give it quite a zap!
LANDO   We fly with haste! Red Group, Gold Group, form up
             And follow me! Today rebellion shall   30
             Have reason to exult! Our enemies
             Shall soon be vanquish'd! O what triumph shall
             Be ours when this great Death Star its own death
             Doth undergo. Three things shall be achiev'd
             Thereby. The first shall be a victory   35
             For our Rebellion—all the fervent hopes
             Of these past years attain'd in one swift stroke.
             The second benefit of Death Star's end
             Is freedom and security for all
             Within the galaxy—no more oppress'd   40
             By evil tyrants, people shall once more

Be free to dwell in possibility.
And finally, the third result of this
Great Death Star's fall shall be the rising up
Of all whose pasts conceal some awful guilt,   45
Some aspect of their lives that brings regret.
I speak of my own past—you all know well
How I betray'd my friend when th'Empire forc'd
My hand. And e'en that friend, good Han, hath through
Rebellion's cause found purpose he had ne'er   50
Imagin'd. In this battle we fight not
To merely terminate an enemy—
Full many of us rebels seek the bliss,
The balm and healing of redemption's touch.
So let it be, my noble comrades all: 55
Fight now for the Rebellion, fight for all
Who dwell within our galaxy, and fight
Most ardently, indeed, for your own souls.
Thus shall we raise those who by Empire's might
Have died, and forth from their celestial graves   60
Shall they ascend and with a rebel's voice
Cry "Havoc!" and let slip the dogs of war!

WEDGE   Well spoken! I fly in for rebels' gain!
NIEN   N'tiya tih.
LANDO   —We fly with thee, good Wedge:
Inside the station, t'ward the centermost.   65
TIE fighters follow us adroitly in—
Mark well how they do come behind anon.
We must outrun them e'en as we approach
The place where we shall strike the Death Star's core.
WEDGE   Form up, good lads, and stay alert. We could   70
Within this tiny shaft lose space with haste.

LANDO   This passage is a narrow path indeed.
               If we can but maneuver cunningly,
               We shall escape the Death Star with our lives
               And, what is more, our hop'd-for victory.   75
               I prithee, pilots all, attend my words:
               Lock all thy weapons to the largest source
               Of power, which should be the generator.
                    [An Imperial pilot strikes Rebel Pilot #1.

PILOT 1   Alas, friends, I am hit, and go to die!
                              [Rebel Pilot 1 dies.

LANDO   I would not even one more pilot lose   80
               Who under my command doth fly herein.
               Pay heed, all: separate by diff'rent paths
               And fly toward the surface. See if you
               Can draw a few TIE fighters thither, too.
               This is the surest hope for our success   85
               Against the Death Star and its minions.

PILOT 2   —Aye,
               Thou speakest well, Gold Leader. We'll obey.
                    [The rebels inside the Death Star separate.
                         Some exit, pursued by Imperial troops,
                            leaving only Lando, Nien Nunb, and
                                   Wedge Antilles inside the shaft.

NIEN   Ah!
                         [The Millennium Falcon scrapes the
                                   wall of the Death Star shaft.

LANDO   —Pardon, Han, I did say not a scratch,
               But did, in this tense moment, break that vow.
               Yet thou and I both know it could be worse—   90
               Our Falcon hath known scrapes in times now past.
               Still, that last brush was far too close; so shall

I try to take more care with borrow'd wings.

ACKBAR   Our fighters must be given yet more time.
This victory is here, within our reach.   95
Thus, concentrate thy pow'r unto the main,
And give the Empire much o'er which to fret.
Within a fiery blaze of weaponry
Let us the Super Star Destroyer wrap.
                    [The rebels outside the Death Star fire on
                         the Super Star Destroyer. Admiral Piett
                         and the Imperial controller are shaken.

CONTROL.   Alas, Sir, our deflector shield is lost!   100
PIETT   Intensify the forward batteries.
Let nothing break the bounds. Intensify,
As well, the forward firing power.
CONTROL.   —Nay!
Too late it is. We die, Sir—O, we die!
                    [The Super Star Destroyer runs into the
                         Death Star, and Admiral Piett and the
                         Imperial controller are killed.

          Enter LUKE SKYWALKER and DARTH VADER on
               balcony, inside the Death Star.

VADER   O Luke, I prithee: render thy support   105
And help me take this mask off.
LUKE   —If I do,
Dear father, thou shalt surely meet thy death.
VADER   Aye. Naught shall stop that now, my son. Just once
Let me look on thee with mine own eyes, Luke—
These eyes that miss'd your mewling newborn face,   110
These eyes that did not see your budding youth,

	These eyes that were not there to see you grow,	
	These eyes that saw thee not when thou wert train'd.	
	I prithee, let these eyes see thee at last.	
	'Twill be a fitting prelude to my death.	115
LUKE	My father, thou dost break my heart in twain.	
	Behold, for thou shalt see thy son, indeed.	

[Luke Skywalker removes Darth Vader's
mask to reveal Anakin Skywalker.

ANAKIN	My misting eyes are nothing like my son's—	
	Thou art so beautiful to me. How strong	
	Thy features, with thy mother's gentle face.	120
	A man thou art, and ev'ry part my son.	
	I never have been prouder, all my life.	

These final moments are pure gift. Now go,
And take thy leave ere this place is destroy'd.

LUKE   But nay, thou shalt come with me. I shall not   125
Desert thee, but shall save thee yet.

ANAKIN   —O, Luke,
Thou hast already done. Thou knewest right—
Thou knewest what I was, for still there was
Some good within me aching to be free.
Tell thy sweet sister this: that thou wert right.

[Anakin Skywalker dies.

LUKE   O Father, fare thee well where'er thou goest,   130
And flights of Jedi sing thee to thy rest!

*[Exit Luke Skywalker, dragging
Anakin Skywalker's body.*

WEDGE   Good General Calrissian, the core
We now have reach'd—'tis here, within my sight.

LANDO   I see it too, Wedge. Let us strike it down!
Approach the power regulator there,   135
Upon the northern tower. Let it burn!

WEDGE   I hear and do obey, Gold Leader. Soon
It shall be done, and then I exit quick.

LANDO   Light up, you vicious beast of evil bent,
You sick creation of humanity's   140
Most wretched and deprivèd sense of right—
Since you could not inspire love, you caus'd fear.
O that a people e'er should such a harsh
And treach'rous weapon like to this create.
For who would make a thing whose only point   145
Is to destroy and murder, maim and kill?
What beings would produce such wickedness
As this: an instrument of pain and death?

Thus I do strike at you with vengeance in
The name of those who have no voice to speak.   150
Farewell, you Star of Death—be now no more!
   [*Wedge Antilles and Lando of Calrissian fire at*
      the Death Star's power generator.

WEDGE 'Tis done, and now we make our great escape.
   Make ready, Admiral, for it shall blow.

ACKBAR Move all the fleet hence, from the Death Star, else
   Our ships may from the grand explosion take   155
   A mighty slap.
     [*The Death Star explodes. Exeunt Lando Calrissian,*
      Nien Nunb, Wedge Antilles, Admiral Ackbar and
      other rebels from the space battle. The rebel crew
      on Endor looks to the sky to see the explosion.

C-3PO —Hurrah! They did it!

CHEWBAC.   —Auugh!

HAN Behold, and all rejoice—the deed is done!
   Yet be ye still, my tongue, for what of Luke?
   [*To Leia:*] Certain I am that Luke was not inside
   When it did perish.

LEIA   —Truly, he was not,   160
   For I can sense he safely doth abide.

HAN [*aside:*] O, shall the love I've shown thus come to naught?
   Her heart doth move toward good Luke, my friend.
   Thus shall I play the noble part, and stay
   Aside whilst their hearts meet, though in the end   165
   It shall undo me. [*To Leia:*] Thou dost love him? Say.

LEIA Be sure I love him.

HAN   —Thus I ascertain'd
   And do respect. Good lady, do not fear:
   When he returns you may be unrestrain'd;

The two of you have my consent sincere.   170

LEIA   Nay, nay, 'tis not as thou dost think, good Han.
         Let not thy visions run amok with thee,
         But hear these words that must fall strangely on
         Thine ears: he is my brother, dost thou see?

                    Enter WICKET.

WICKET   N'yubba, yubba,   175
         Heezur brubba,
         Yoozur luvva,
         Nyubba, nyubba.
                    [Han Solo rises, singing and dancing.
HAN   [*sings:*] O revelation kind, my heart doth swell—
         A'merrily my feet do trip!   180
         My Leia's mine, and I am hers as well.
         Sing ho, sing hi, sing heigh!
         Though Leia and myself did fear the worst,
         A'merrily my feet do trip!
         Good Luke is safe from Death Star's mighty burst. 185
         Sing ho, sing hi, sing heigh!
         We all are safe from that dire threat above—
         A'merrily my feet do trip!
         Thus end our wars with thoughts of blissful love!
         Sing ho, sing hi, sing heigh!   190
         Our rebel crew hath won the victory,
         A'merrily my feet do trip!
         Thus sing together, worthy company!
         Sing ho, sing hi, sing heigh!
                              [Exeunt.

SCENE 4.

The forest moon of Endor.

Enter LUKE SKYWALKER, *with the*
body of ANAKIN SKYWALKER.

LUKE   The fun'ral pyre shall light my father's way
              To glory out beyond the galaxy.
              His final journey shall not be by ship,
              But by the smoke that lifts into the air.
                   [Luke lights the wood on which Anakin's body lies.
              Rise up, my father—take thy closing flight.   5
              Rise up, my father—stretch toward the sun.
              Rise up, my father—man of tragedy,
              Rise up, my father—rise, and thus be free.
              Now is my heart full heavy, burden'd with
              Such muddl'd thoughts that strain my very soul.   10
              Methinks I should be happy, should rejoice
              At our sure victory, the Empire crush'd.
              Yet how can I make merry when the man
              I hardly knew—the father I had wish'd
              For years to meet—is come and gone like wind?   15
              O trick of Fortune, cruel-minded Fate!
              O wherefore mock at all my hope, my life?
              Am I a simple pawn with which thou play'st?
              Or hast thou e'er a purpose had for me?
              But stop thy tongue now, Luke, thou art misled—   20
              Aye, even as I rant I see my fault.
              For why should I blame Fate for thievery
              When it was Fate, indeed, that did decree

THE JEDI DOTH RETURN V, 4

That I would meet my father, that we two
Would reunite with joy ere he did die?   25
Should I not thank the blessèd Fate that knit
This fascinating cord of life for me?
I have seen stars, and space, and battles, too,
Have had adventures grand with noble friends,
And at the last, have met my father. Nay,   30
Not only met, but witness'd his rebirth.
And therefore, I declare with gratitude
That I do thank the Fate that brought me here,

E'en to this tragic pyre on which he's laid.
Now this is sure: whate'er befall me now,   35
I am a better man for having known
The one whose name I bear: e'en Anakin.

Enter HAN SOLO, PRINCESS LEIA, CHEWBACCA, C-3PO, R2-D2,
LANDO OF CALRISSIAN, WEDGE ANTILLES, ADMIRAL ACKBAR,
other REBELS, *and* EWOKS, *celebrating. Enter* CHORUS.

CHORUS   The rebels meet with joy to celebrate,
            Their singing and their music fill the air.
            The Empire is defeated in its hate,   40
            And now Rebellion takes its respite rare.
            The Jedi Luke looks up and sees three men—
            Their countenances shine in bluish light—
            'Tis Yoda, Obi-Wan, and Anakin
            Who come e'en from the grave to share this night.   45
            All who did fight together come as one,
            And give unto each other their embrace.
            O'er this scene merry falls the setting sun;
            Not till 'tis day shall they the future face.
HAN   Our mouths with mirth and laughter raise a din,   50
            Our feet with glee and triumph stomp the ground,
            Our bodies are awake and full of life,
            Our souls are heal'd from Empire's treachery.
LEIA   New hope did guide our first adventures, aye,
            Until the Empire harshly struck us back,   55
            But then our noble Jedi hath return'd
            And all ensur'd our victory was won.
LUKE   We stop, e'en as our epic play doth end,
            To thank thee for thy gracious company.

Our star wars now are ended, for a time—   60
The song of peace bursts forth in perfect rhyme.

        [All freeze as R2-D2 takes center stage.

R2-D2   Even thus, our tale is finish'd.
Pardon if your hope's diminish'd—
If you did not find the sequel
Satisfying. If unequal   65
Our keen play is unto others,
Do not part in anger, brothers.
Ears, attend: I know surprises,
Visions of all shapes and sizes.
In some other times and places   70
It may be Rebellion faces
Certain dangers that may sever
Our strong bonds that held us ever.
Mayhap something compromising,
Even like an Empire Rising.   75
Thus present I our conclusion:
Hint of Fate, or Fool's illusion?

        [Exeunt omnes.

END.

AFTERWORD.

How do you solve a problem like the Ewoks? In *Return of the Jedi*, the Ewoks say things like "gunda" and "yubnub!" but for *The Jedi Doth Return* I wanted to make their speech distinctive without resorting to a device I had used before. After all, the Ewoks are one of very few types of foreign-language speaking creatures introduced in *Return of the Jedi* (Jabba and his language first appear in the scenes that were added to *A New Hope*). They're known for their unique way of communicating, so I wanted to do something special for them. I didn't want them to speak English (like Salacious Crumb), I didn't want them to sing (like the Rancor, or the Ugnaughts from *William Shakespeare's The Empire Striketh Back*), and I didn't want them simply to speak in an untranslated foreign language (like R2's beeps, or Jabba's Huttese). Instead, I wanted their speech to feel unique. Ultimately, I had them talk in short lines of verse with an AABA rhyme scheme, with dashes of almost a pidgin English thrown in. For example, here is my version of Wicket's first line when he finds Leia unconscious in the forest:

> A buki buki,
> Luki, luki,
> Issa creecher,
> Nuki, nuki!

This starts off sounding like a normal Ewok line—as often as possible, my first line of the Ewok quatrains uses the Ewokese spoken in the film. Then the second and third lines are in quasi-English: "Look, look, it's a creature" is the translation here. The final line is there simply to rhyme with the first. I admit: this structure isn't very

Shakespearean. But I think it meets my goal of making the Ewoks' speech distinctive, interesting, and even a bit intelligible. (As a side note, one of the most fun things about working with Lucasfilm is that someone will check your Huttese, your Ewokese, and any other alien tongue from the films. Yes, official versions exist of every language you hear in the *Star Wars* trilogy.)

Speaking of characters who speak distinctively, let's talk about R2-D2. The plucky little droid is the fool of the trilogy—a fool not in the modern sense but in the Shakespearean sense: a knowing presence who aids the action even though he seems somewhat simple. R2's asides in English from *William Shakespeare's Star Wars* through *William Shakespeare's The Jedi Doth Return* situate him as such. That's why he delivers the last line of the trilogy, speaking of what has been and what may be to come (bonus points for finding the Easter egg hidden in those final verses). That said, I decided Jabba's court should have its own fool, who of course had to be Salacious Crumb. He speaks in English throughout *William Shakespeare's The Jedi Doth Return*, commenting on the action and aware at every moment of how the players around him are positioned. It's no surprise that in *Return of the Jedi*, it's R2 who finally gets the best of Crumb—the two fools duke it out, and the better fool wins. (Who's more foolish—the fool or the fool who electrocutes him?)

Writing the *William Shakespeare's Star Wars* trilogy meant I had more and more ground rules—of my own making—to remember with each volume. In *Verily, A New Hope*, I established the vocabulary of R2-D2's beeps and Chewbacca's growls, and the fact that R2 speaks English when he is alone, and the Shakespearean devices of rhyming couplets at the ends of scenes, and of course the iambic pentameter throughout. . . . In *The Empire Striketh Back*, I added Yoda speaking in haiku, Han and Leia speaking in rhyming quatrains to each other when alone (like Romeo and Juliet), and Boba Fett speaking in prose.

By the time of this third installment, keeping these rules in mind while adding new ones—the Ewoks' manner of speaking, Admiral Ackbar's line endings, and so forth—was quite a juggling act. But what fun it has been immersing myself in this universe that I love and having an opportunity to put words into the mouths of characters I have known for decades.

As I mentioned in my afterword to *The Empire Striketh Back*, *Return of the Jedi* is my favorite of the three original movies. I know *Empire* is widely considered the best of the trilogy, and the older I get, the more I understand why. But I have a soft spot in my heart for *Jedi*. It was the first of the trilogy that I saw in a movie theater. I vividly remember being six years old, watching the film with my uncle Norman who sat in the row behind me and translated the dialogue into Japanese for my aunt Sooja. (What's the Japanese word for "sarlacc"?) Furthermore, growing up, we had *The Making of a Saga* on VHS, which covered the whole trilogy but focused primarily on *Return of the Jedi*, which cemented its primary status in my young heart. I've always loved the Jabba sequence, and although the Ewoks' charm has grown a little thin now that I'm an adult, I still love the movie as a whole. So writing this final book of the trilogy was, as with the first two, a real joy.

Of course, *Return of the Jedi* is where the story of Darth Vader comes full circle. The character development of Anakin Skywalker/ Darth Vader—from Episode I through Episode VI—is a triumph of modern cinema. Vader's transformation in *Return of the Jedi* comes across as both believable and natural, as if written by Fate, and that's true whether you start watching at Episode IV or at Episode I. *Return of the Jedi* has more depth than people tend to acknowledge, due in large part to the cathartic final scenes between Darth Vader and Luke Skywalker. Luke realizes how close he comes to the dark side, as he considers his own robotic hand and the severed limb of his father, which Luke himself cut off in a moment of fury. Darth Vader realizes he has a decision to make: save his son, or remain a slave to his Emperor. We see him make that choice in the most dramatic way possible, as he grasps the Emperor and casts him into the abyss to his doom. Those two events—the separate awakenings of Luke Skywalker and Darth Vader—are masterful film moments, and utterly Shakespearean. Darth Vader realizes in the end that it is his son, not his Emperor, who matters, just as King Lear realizes before his death that Cordelia loved him better than Goneril and Regan ever could. These are weighty moments. I knew that even when I was six.

Thank you, all of you who have entered the world of the *William Shakespeare's Star Wars* trilogy. This has been a special journey for me; I hope it has been for you as well.

May the Force be with you, always.

ACKNOWLEDGMENTS.

Once again, there are many to whom I am deeply grateful. This book is dedicated to my parents, Beth and Bob Doescher, and my brother Erik, who have encouraged and supported me more than I deserve. I grew up in a family where *Star Wars* was part of the fabric of our lives, and for that I am grateful.

Thank you to the wonderful people of Quirk Books: editors Jason Rekulak and Rick Chillot, publicity manager Nicole De Jackmo, social media manager Eric Smith, and the rest of the gang. Thank you to my agent, Adriann Ranta, for her support throughout the trilogy and for looking ahead with me. Thank you to Jennifer Heddle at Lucasfilm for being a delight to work with, and to illustrator Nicolas Delort for making the pages dance.

Continued thanks to my college professor and friend Murray Biggs, who reviewed all three manuscripts to enrich the Shakespearean pastiche. Thank you to my friend Josh Hicks, who listened to every idea and offered insightful, helpful feedback. Thank you to dear college friends Heidi Altman, Chris Martin, Naomi Walcott, and Ethan Youngerman, and high school friends (and their spouses) Travis Boeh, Chris Buehler, Erin Buehler, Nathan Buehler, Katie Downing, Marian Hammond, Anne Huebsch, Michael Morrill, Tara Schuster, Ben Wire, and Sarah Woodburn.

Thank you to everyone else: Audu Besmer, Jane Bidwell, Jeff and Caryl Creswell, Ken Evers-Hood, Mark Fordice, Chris Frimoth, Alana Garrigues, Brian Heron, Jim and Nancy Hicks, Apricot and David Irving, Doree Jarboe, Alexis Kaushansky, Rebecca Lessem, Bobby Lopez, Andrea Martin, Bruce McDonald, Joan and Grady Miller, Jim Moiso, Janice Morgan, Dave Nieuwstraten,

Julia Rodriguez-O'Donnell, Scott Roehm, Larry Rothe, Steve Weeks, Ryan Wilmot, and members of the 501st Legion.

Finally, to my spouse, Jennifer, and our boys, Liam and Graham: thank you beyond rhyme, beyond meter, beyond words.

COLLECT
ALL THREE VOLUMES
IN THE
WILLIAM SHAKESPEARE'S
STAR WARS TRILOGY.

SONNET 1983

"To Http or Not to Http . . ."

Stout Jabba has receiv'd his just desert,
Old Anakin and Luke are reconcil'd,
The rebels do their victory assert—
A better end Saint George could not have styl'd.
And thus, dear friends, our charms are all o'erthrown;
The credits roll with sound of drum and fife.
But just as *Star Wars* has tales yet unknown,
Beyond these pages these three books have life.
So let thy fervent joy increase online
As thou with haste the **book trailers** pursue.
The **educators' guides** for free are thine,
Or read o'er **Ian Doescher's interview.**
With all good speed to **Quirk Books' site** get thee,
And ne'er forget thou this book trilogy.